ROLLS-ROYCE

ROLLS-ROYCE

THE BEST CAR IN THE WORLD

John Heilig *with* Reg Abbiss

CHARTWELL
BOOKS, INC.

A QUINTET BOOK

Published by Chartwell Books
A Division of Book Sales, Inc.
114, Northfield Avenue
Edison, New Jersey 08837

This edition produced for sale in the U.S.A., its territories, and dependencies only.

Copyright © 1999 Quintet Publishing Limited.

ISBN 0 7858 1051 x

This book was designed and produced by
Quintet Publishing Limited
6 Blundell Street
London N7 9BH

Creative Director: Richard Dewing
Art Director: Simon Daley
Project Editors: Clare Hubbard, Laura Price
Editor: Ian Penberthy

Typeset in Great Britain by Central Southern Typesetters, Eastbourne
Manufactured in Hong Kong by Regent Publishing Services Ltd.
Printed in Singapore by Star Standard Industries (Pte) Ltd.

CONTENTS

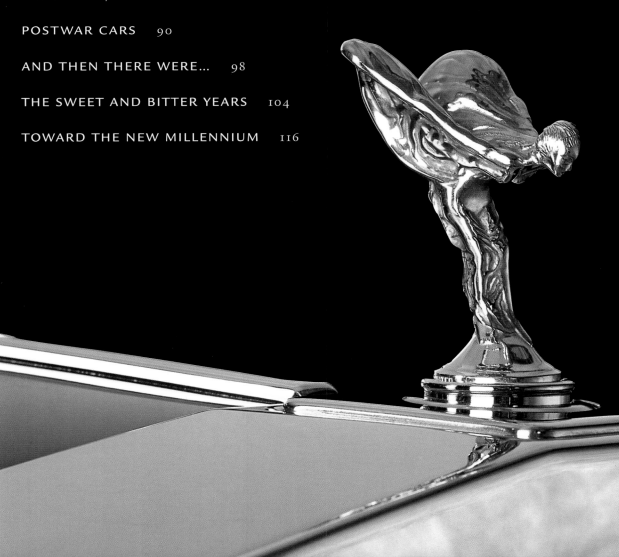

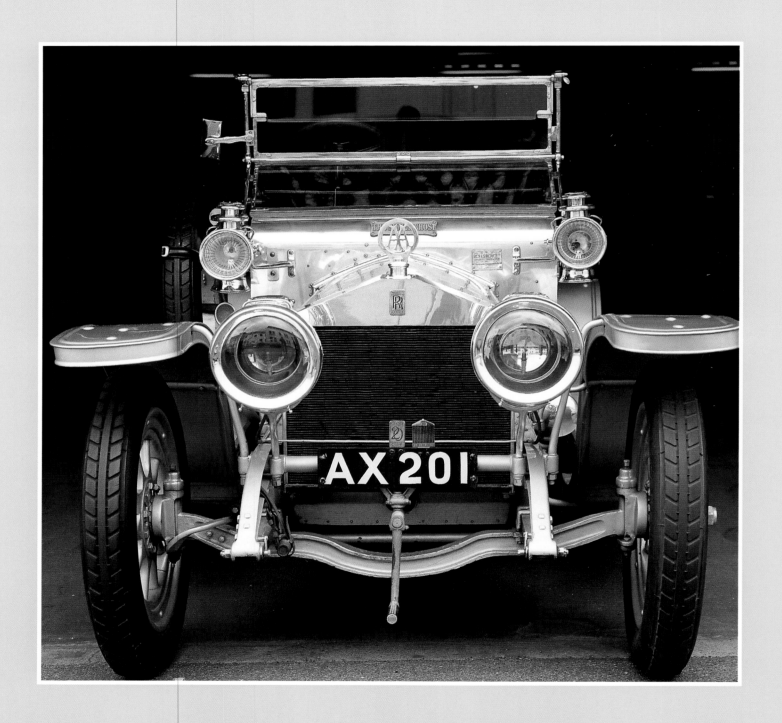

INTRODUCTION

Rolls-Royce automobiles became known as "the best cars in the world" from the first time a magazine editor had an opportunity to drive one. Henry Royce's devotion to quality, and Charles Rolls's successful promotions showed the world that here was a vehicle that was far ahead of anything else that could be made at the time.

What is interesting about Rolls-Royce is that the company has continued to stress quality in the products it builds. Where mass production by robots may produce a vehicle that is exactly like the one before it and after it, the hand crafting and constant inspection that Rolls-Royce puts into its automobiles leads to virtually unnoticeable differences, but also guarantees a constantly higher quality of production.

Someone once said that Rolls-Royce puts a premium on antiquity. Today, cars aren't built with matched leather hides in the seats and perfectly matched veneers on the dash. It's too expensive and time-consuming. But expense and time have never been the controlling factors in building Rolls-Royce cars; building them right has been.

For years, Rolls-Royce cars were powered by an ancient six-cylinder engine. Only relatively recently has a V-8 engine found its way under the long hood. The BMW-designed V-12 is the latest surprise, and it gives the car performance worthy of its styling.

As we enter a new millennium, the future of Rolls-Royce seems in doubt. The auto division of the company was purchased from its parent, Vickers, by Volkswagen, of all organizations. There is an agreement to transfer the company to BMW early in the twenty-first century, but for the world's most elegant car to be built by a manufacturer of German economy cars comes as a shock. Of course, VW also builds Audi cars, and for years was under the tutelage of Ferdinand Porsche, but still it is a shock.

The VW purchase did infuse Rolls-Royce with the necessary cash to continue operating the way it had done for years. This is the critical point: Rolls-Royce will not change under Volkswagen leadership. If anything, new minds will be put in charge of design and engineering that may make Rolls-Royce cars even better.

It is obvious from the last two chapters of this book that I had considerable assistance in its creation. At one time, Reg Abbiss was my point of contact at Rolls-Royce United States, in his capacity as Vice President of Communications. I dare say there are few people who know as much about modern Rolls-Royces as he does. That is why I asked him to write those chapters. In addition, he provided the answers to some sticky questions posed by the earlier chapters.

Finally, of course, I could not have completed this work without the cooperation and love of my wife, Florence. As 1998 turned into 1999, I was busy working on two books and the program for the New York International Automobile Show, as well as holding down a full-time job with an advertising agency. Florence would see me for dinner, then I would hie up to the office and pound away on the computer on one of the three projects, all of which had similar deadlines. That any of them got done was a miracle. Fortunately, she had the support of our three children, Susan, Sharon and Laura, and their husbands, which made it all worthwhile.

JOHN HEILIG • MAY 1999

I MR ROYCE & MR ROLLS

Henry Royce's first 10 hp car, in bare chassis form, shows its basic simplicity. It was powered by a 1.8-liter two-cylinder engine.

Henry Royce's dedication to building the most refined automobile he possibly could was at the core of the Rolls-Royce legend.

Charles Stewart Rolls, in contrast to Royce, was a dilettante playboy who contributed financial backing for Rolls to design and build automobiles.

The 1905 10 hp Rolls-Royce was a massive machine, driven by just two cylinders. Here, life-long employee Harry Fleck sits at the wheel.

THE HEROES OF THE EARLY YEARS OF THE AUTOMOBILE ARE STILL HONORED BY THE CARS THAT BEAR THEIR NAMES: HENRY FORD, RANSOM E. OLDS, DAVID DUNBAR BUICK, WALTER CHRYSLER, THE DODGE BROTHERS. GOTTLIEB DAIMLER AND KARL BENZ LOANED THEIR NAMES TO DAIMLER-BENZ EVEN THOUGH THE CARS THAT COMPANY BUILDS ARE NOW CALLED MERCEDES. SO IT IS WITH HENRY ROYCE, WHO BUILT THREE CARS IN 1904, JOINED WITH THE HONORABLE CHARLES S. ROLLS SHORTLY THEREAFTER, AND FROM THEN ON BUILT WHAT MAY ARGUABLY BE CONSIDERED THE BEST CARS IN THE WORLD. THE PARTNERSHIP BETWEEN ROYCE AND ROLLS WAS FOUNDED TO BUILD AND MARKET JUST THAT—THE BEST CAR THAT COULD POSSIBLY BE BUILT AT THE TIME. AND, WHILE THERE HAVE BEEN A FEW POTHOLES IN THE ROAD THE FOUNDERS CHOSE, IN GENERAL THEY AND THEIR HEIRS AT ROLLS-ROYCE MOTOR CARS HAVE SUCCEEDED ADMIRABLY IN THEIR EFFORTS.

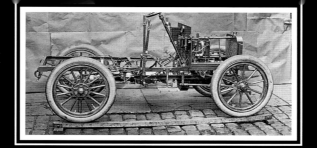

ROLLS ROYCE
1905
——
B.I

ABOVE • Here, C.S. Rolls is shown at the wheel of a Royce car with the Duke of Connaught in the passenger seat.

MR HENRY ROYCE

We begin our story with Henry Royce, because it was his devotion to quality and the production of a superior product that made what followed possible.

Frederick Henry Royce was born near Peterborough in east-central England in 1863, the son of a miller. His first jobs were selling newspapers. At the age of 14 he became an apprentice at the locomotive works of the Great Northern Railway. Three years later he left to work at a machine-tool company in Leeds in Yorkshire. Later he worked for an electric-power company in London. He was still in his teens and never did complete the apprenticeship program he began when he was 14.

After the power company, Royce was hired as a technical adviser to the Lancaster Maxim and Western Electric Company. However, he could not settle and, still restless, before 1890 he was in business with a partner, Ernest Claremont, manufacturing a variety of electrical products, from light-bulb sockets through doorbells to small generators.

It was in the quality of their generators and electric motors that Royce and Claremont earned their reputations. The two partners even began earning profits. Royce bought a small house and was married, but the strain of working 18 to 20 hours a day forced the couple to live apart from 1920 onwards, although they stayed in touch with each other. The pressure also took its toll on Royce's health.

Royce Ltd was incorporated in 1894 with Royce, Claremont, and a bookkeeper, John deLooze, listed as partners.

The company expanded into building construction cranes. Even though their electric cranes were more expensive than the steam-powered cranes then in vogue, the quality and reliability of the Royce cranes was such that it brought them a stream of orders.

It was the age of the automobile in England. Where this new contraption had caught on in Germany and France, it had been slow to cross the Channel. Henry Royce was naturally fascinated with the automobile and decided to perform some experiments. Fortunately, he did not decide to apply his knowledge of electric power to the automobile but chose instead to investigate the problems of burning the fuel–air mixture in the cylinder of an internal-combustion chamber. He bought a French Decauville as his rolling laboratory.

Very few people today remember the Decauville after it died in 1911, but it earned its place in history as the vehicle that inspired Henry Royce.

As was his wont, Royce immediately began to improve just about everything he could on the Decauville. His attention to quality production methods with his motors and generators showed him that no such care was taken in building the French car. He recognized that the automobile—at least as represented by the example he was working with—suffered from the fact that no one had measured the stresses acting on the engine, the frame, or the body.

TOP • Only 19 two-cylinder Royce and Rolls-Royce cars were built, three Royces in 1904 and 16 Rolls-Royces up to 1906. All developed an estimated 12 hp.

BOTTOM • The early two-cylinder Royce car had a purposeful radiator grille. The classic Rolls-Royce Grecian-style grille was still in the future.

As the historian Halwart Schrader has noted in *Rolls-Royce Cars and Bentley from 1931*,

"He knew from experience that the effectiveness, dependability, noise and vibration levels, operating cost and longevity of a machine are fully dependent on tolerances. That led him to the conclusion that high precision was also the central, and most vital, element in the construction of a quality motor car."

Interestingly, Henry Leland and his son Wilfred in the United States reached similar conclusions as they set out to build Cadillac cars.

Sometime in 1903, Royce decided to build three cars of his own. The first was completed and was running (perfectly) on April 1, 1904. As the historian Phil May noted in *20 Silver Ghosts*, "The car did not really represent an engineering breakthrough in the field, but was so refined, and so well thought out, that it was quite possibly the finest motorcar in operation at that time."

Physically, the three Royce cars resembled the Decauville. Since Royce's rationale for building the cars was not to begin production of his own marque, but rather to test his theories of applying high-precision manufacturing techniques to automobile production, there was no reason to build anything other than a two-seater Decauville clone. He just wanted to build it better.

Royce had firm views on the need for quality and a Victorian fancy for expressing his aims in stirring phrases. "Small things make perfection, but perfection is no small thing," he once said. "Whatever is rightly done, however humble, is noble." He also noted that "the quality remains long after the price is forgotten."

Even though the Royce resembled the Decauville, it carried a Royce carburetor and muffler, gearboxes and axles, all built in the Royce factory.

BOTTOM LEFT • **Rolls was one of the first Britons to fly with Wilbur Wright. Here he pilots a Wright Flyer.**

BOTTOM RIGHT • **C.S. Rolls sold and repaired French and Belgian cars in this facility at Lillie Hall.**

Charles Stuart Rolls led a different life. He was born in London in 1877, the third son of Lord Llangattock. Like William K. Vanderbilt Jr on the other side of the Atlantic, he had sufficient financial resources to pursue anything that interested him. He also had the benefit of a Cambridge engineering education.

Rolls bought a Peugeot in France and at the age of 19 began racing it. He also drove a Mors in the 1901 Paris-to-Berlin race.

Rolls was part of a group that founded Britain's first auto show in 1895. He also began a company to import French and Belgian cars in 1902. His partner was Claude G. Johnson, who had been secretary of the Automobile Club of Great Britain and Ireland (ACGBI) since it was

founded in 1897. Johnson helped Rolls establish a service-and-repair shop at Lillie Hall. When the business didn't achieve a solid financial footing, Rolls looked to Royce's new cars to replace the poor-selling Panhard.

Ever the adventurer, Rolls would go on to fly with Wilbur Wright and would be the first person to cross the English Channel both ways by plane. He set a world land-speed record (also like Vanderbilt) and was an avid balloonist. According to Lord Montagu of Beaulieu, Rolls was one of the founders of the Royal Aero Club. By the time he had reached the age of 33 he was rated a national hero and was beloved by the British public. He would meet an early death in July 1910 when the plane he was flying crashed during an air show at the

Bournemouth Fortnight to celebrate the southern resort's centenary.

When the two famous names were brought together by Royce's business manager in Manchester (see box), here was a true "odd couple": the young rash Rolls, then 27, and the careful, studious Royce, 41. The two had lunch and decided to go for a ride in Edmunds's Royce car. Rolls must have enjoyed the ride.

Back in London, Rolls took Claude Johnson for a ride in the car in the middle of the night through the deserted streets of the city. Johnson was similarly impressed with the car, and on December 23, 1904, an agreement was signed through which C. S. Rolls and Company had exclusive rights to sell Royce cars. The agreement also stipulated that, henceforth, the cars would be sold under a new name: Rolls-Royce. In March 1906, Rolls-Royce Limited was formed with an initial capital of £60,000.

Paris E. Singer, heir to the Singer sewing-machine fortune, bought the first Rolls-Royce. This car was also shown at an exhibition in Olympia, west London. It was greeted with almost universal acclaim. Orders came rushing in to the offices of C. S. Rolls & Co.

Royce worked day and night to complete two cars based on his 10-horsepower design. One was used for demonstration runs, the other for show. Royce also built 15-horsepower and 20-horsepower models, as well as a six-cylinder engine. The two- and four-cylinder cars were taken out of production in 1908 and the six-cylinder remained the engine of choice for Rolls-Royce until 1959, with certain notable exceptions.

The car on display in Paris was identical to the experimental car Royce had built, with one exception. The show car had a radiator in the shape of a Greek temple, with the names Rolls and Royce inside a horizontal oval. Royce never indicated why he chose this shape for a radiator, but it has survived as long as the car has. Over the years the shape has been "morphed" by making it lower and wider, but the essential design remains.

Rolls-Royce won a prize for "Elegance and Comfort" at the 1904 Paris show. Everyone who saw the car on demonstration runs was impressed by the quiet engine and its freedom from vibration.

Rolls-Royce produced 16 10-horsepower cars between 1904 and 1906. All were essentially identical to the first

AN HISTORIC MEETING

Claude Johnson built his reputation as an elder statesman of motoring, who was remembered for his work as secretary of the ACGBI, for his organization of the Thousand Miles Trial and for his diplomacy in acting as a go-between among the various automobile associations and the press.

Johnson had heard about the cars that Henry Royce had built and thought they might make an interesting product for Rolls's dealership. Henry Edmunds, owned the third Royce car and suggested to Johnson that Royce and Rolls should get together. The two met at the Midland Hotel in Manchester, now the Holiday Inn Crowne Plaza.

Edmunds was also a founder–member of the ACGBI and had known Rolls for some time. He met Royce when he bought some shares in his company. Royce asked him to try

the experimental 10 horsepower car and Edmunds liked it and thought it would meet with public acceptance. He also knew that Rolls was looking for a replacement for the Panhard and decided to arrange a meeting between Royce and Rolls.

Manchester was chosen as the venue because Royce didn't want to be too far from his workshops. Rolls agreed because he was intrigued about the possibilities.

Royce. There were engine modifications, notably a shift from a two-bearing to a three-bearing crankshaft. Royce electrical ignition systems also made their way inside the car, and a fan was mounted behind the radiator to force cooling air through it.

Only six 15-horsepower cars were produced. This was a three-cylinder car with the same cylinder dimensions as the 10-horsepower two-cylinder, but with an extra cylinder. Rolls-Royce ceased production almost immediately, but not because of lack of demand. Since the larger six-cylinder engine was similar to the two- and four-cylinder engines (all three were built from pairs of identical cylinders) the odd-numbered three-cylinder simply didn't fit in.

According to Lord Montagu, it was Rolls's name that was stressed in the early ads. Royce Ltd received second billing with the words "Works, Manchester" in small

type. The 1905 catalog was 100 pages long and contained comprehensive details of the full range of cars, testimonials from owners and biographies of Rolls and Johnson—with no mention of Royce.

In that catalog were two primary Rolls-Royce cars, the 20-horsepower four-cylinder and a six-cylinder Thirty. There was a 10-horsepower "twin," a 15-horsepower three-cylinder, two versions of the Twenty, and the Thirty. A V-8 was added in 1906, but the Twenty was the best seller.

At the 1905 London Motor Show, the 20-horsepower model was the center of the display. The four-cylinder engine of the Twenty had the same stroke (five inches) as the two- and three-cylinder models, but the bore was increased to four inches, giving a total displacement of 4.1 liters. There were now five phosphor-bronze bearings supporting the crankshaft.

CLOCKWISE FROM TOP: In 1906, the six-cylinder 30 hp replaced the 20 hp. Here, C.S. Rolls is shown at the wheel.

This 20 hp Rolls-Royce, with a Roi des Belges body by Barker, had a 4.1-liter engine and could attain 60 mph.

Rolls-Royce only built six three-cylinder 15 hp models. Production was halted to concentrate on the four-cylinder model.

It was possible to have a closed body built on the 30 hp chassis, as in this model. Note that the driver was still exposed to the elements in the landaulet.

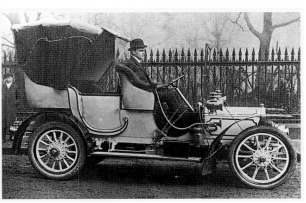

RACING TO SUCCESS

With a new toy to drive and a financial interest in its success, Rolls promoted the Rolls-Royce cars tirelessly. He entered the cars in the Tourist Trophy races on the Isle of Man in 1905 and 1906, since motor racing was banned in England at the time.

The object of the TT races was "the improvement of motorcars of a type which is useful to the ordinary purchaser." The 1905 race alone attracted a list of the leading car manufacturers that included Napier, Daimler, Wolseley, Siddeley, Spyker, Star, Argyll, White, Renault, Darracq, and Peugeot, as well as Vauxhall and Humber. An American car, the Cadillac, was also entered in the race.

Rolls drove a reconnaissance run on the Isle of Man in an open-bodied Twenty and recommended optimum gear ratios to Royce to obtain maximum fuel economy. The cars would have to average 22.5 miles per gallon if they completed the four laps of the 52-mile course. Two Rolls-Royce cars were entered in the 1905 race, a standard Twenty driven by Percy Northey and the modified car for Rolls with its cylinder bore increased by 5 mm to 100 mm.

Rolls was the first car off the line as the cars coasted downhill. He failed in his attempt to engage third gear. He tried his "sprinting gear" and failed again. Then he tried third again. There was a loud crack, and the Rolls-Royce coasted to a stop.

Northey, on the other hand, had little problem with his standard Twenty. He circulated at a steady pace and had the fastest lap, 34.1 mph. His was the first car to finish the race. Victory, however, went to the Arrol-Johnson of J. S. Napier, who had averaged 33.9 mph to Northey's 33.7 mph. Rolls protested, complaining of

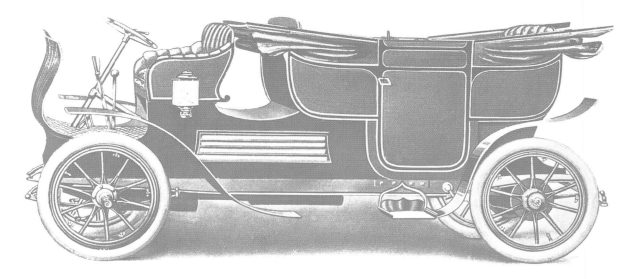

sabotage because he claimed he found some broken loose nuts in the bottom of his gearbox, but the protest was disallowed.

In the 1906 TT the rules were changed slightly. Weight restrictions were abandoned and the fuel economy was raised to 25 mpg. It was still a reliability run, since the cars had to cover a measured half-mile in top gear at 12 mph and undertake a stop and restart on a gradient of one in six.

Rolls and Northey both practiced with wooden wheels on their cars. Rolls remembered, however, that the cars with wooden wheels often broke them on hard cornering, so he spent £40 on improvements. In the race they used wire wheels.

Rolls had better luck at the start: Northey broke down on the first lap. This time, Rolls emerged victorious, saying, "I had nothing to do but sit there and wait till the car got to the finish." He averaged 39.3 mph for four laps to the second-placed Paul Bablot in a Berliet, who averaged 35.4 mph. Immediately after the race, Rolls left for the first Gordon Bennett Balloon Cup race in Paris.

Success brought expansion. Royce's factory on Cooke Street, Manchester, was before too long too small to handle production. In 1908 he moved to a larger factory farther south in Derby. It was from the Derby factory that the 40/50 Silver Ghost cars that established Rolls-Royce's reputation as the best cars in the world came. The first Ghosts stayed in production until 1925, a fitting tribute to their reliability and luxuriousness.

Two other pre-Silver Ghost Rolls-Royces deserve mention. One is the six-cylinder 30-horsepower and the other the V-8-engined Legalimit. Only three Legalimits were manufactured by Rolls Royce, while 37 six-cylinder cars reached production.

The first-production six-cylinder car, that Royce used as his personal car, was shown at the 1905 New York Automobile Show. The engine was simply the natural extension of the two- and four-cylinder models, with three sets of two cylinders, yielding a displacement of 6.2 liters. However, with the now-longer crankshaft, seven bearings were required to eliminate vibrations.

This model was offered in two wheelbase lengths, 116.5 and 118 inches. The long-wheelbase chassis was for a seven-passenger body, usually built by Barker.

Royce decided on the V-8 configuration because it was shorter, more rigid, and would have a lower profile than inline engines. He also decided to build a car with no discernible hood, thereby making the V-8-powered car look like an electric car. Unfortunately, by this time long hoods had been the accepted design style for elegant cars. This was alleged to be one of Claude Johnson's few mistakes.

The V-8 engine had a bore and stroke of 3.25 inches for a displacement of 3.5 liters. Output was estimated at 40 horsepower.

It achieved its name "Legalimit" because it was capable of maintaining the then maximum speed of 20 mph in direct drive. It could maintain this speed up hills and down hills by setting the hand throttle.

ABOVE • **Rolls-Royce built three V-8-engined Legalimits in 1905-1906. It was so named because it could maintain the 20 mph speed limit in top gear all day using an early form of cruise control.**

OPPOSITE TOP • **Percy Northey drove this four cylinder 20 hp Rolls-Royce to a second-place finish in the 1905 Tourist Trophy race on the Isle of Man.**

OPPOSITE BOTTOM • **C.S. Rolls won the 1906 Tourist Trophy race. He said, "I had nothing to do but sit there . . ."**

TOP • **Rolls-Royce cars were initially manufactured in this factory at Cook Street, Manchester.**

BOTTOM • **The Cook Street factory, with its wooden floor, was previously used to manufacture Royce electric cranes.**

Royce became ill in 1911. The fate of the firm was threatened as well as Royce's life because he was the engineering genius behind the cars and was the mainstay of the firm. Claude Johnson suggested a tour of the Continent and the Near East. Royce's strength returned. On the way back to England, the two stopped in Le Canadel in the South of France. When Royce remarked to Johnson that it would be a nice place to build a house, Johnson put an architect to work and had a villa built for Royce. Royce moved to Le Canadel and never again set foot in the Rolls-Royce factory, although his ideas and drawings were sent to Derby frequently. When a second illness struck Royce, a hospital in England diagnosed it as a malignant tumor. An operation left him a semi-invalid.

Claude Johnson died in 1926, remembered as the man who ceaselessly promoted Rolls-Royce cars and who saved the company by saving Henry Royce's life.

Royce was made a baronet in 1931. His official title was Sir Frederick Henry Royce, Bart., OBE, MIME. He died on April 22, 1933.

EARLY BODYWORK

Until the late 1940's, bodywork for Rolls-Royce was supplied by a number of custom coach building house. Barker & Company of North Kensington fitted bodies to most of the early cars. Chassis would be delivered from Manchester without lights and other fittings. In 1913 a state limousine built for the Nizam of Hyderabad which had a raised throne on gold mounts with four collapsible seats for his attendants.

Soon after Royce's death the intertwined R and R was changed from the original red to black and the frame around the rectangle was also changed to black. The instruction to change the colours was given by Royce himself before his death.

The first competitive outing for these cars was in 1913. The Ghosts thoroughly defeated all the other entrants in the Alpenfahrt, a durability and speed test around the Austrian Alps. Rolls-Royce's effortless performance earned them the accolade "the best motor cars in the world" from *The Motor*.

Britain's royal family has always appreciated Rolls-Royce quality. The first member of British royalty to own a Rolls-Royce was the Duke of Windsor. Queen Elizabeth II owns five official Rolls-Royce cars, all with a solid silver statuette of St George and the Dragon replacing the flying lady on the hood.

Other heads of state also appreciated the cars, particularly in Russia. Czar Nicholas II owned two Silver Ghosts. Lenin owned four and even Stalin and Leonid Brezhnev drove and rode in Rolls-Royces during their years of premiership.

ABOVE LEFT • Even the champion of the proletariat, Vladimir Lenin, owned and drove a Rolls-Royce in front of the Kremlin.

ABOVE • During World War I, King George V toured the Western Front in a Rolls-Royce Silver Ghost.

CLOCKWISE FROM TOP:
1910 40/50 Roi des Belges spare
tyre retainer

Wheel center and spokes of the 1910
40/50 Roi des Belges

Detail showing the identification plate
of the 1910 40/50 Roi des Belges

1910 40/50 Roi des Belges

IF THE INITIAL REPUTATION OF ROLLS-ROYCE WAS

EARNED THROUGH THE FIRST TWENTY AND THIRTY

MODELS, IT WAS ENSURED WITH THE RELEASE OF THE

FIRST GHOST MODELS IN 1906. THESE CARS WERE NOT

ORIGINALLY CALLED SILVER GHOSTS OR EVEN GHOSTS. IN

THE STANDARD ROLLS-ROYCE HIERARCHY, THE CARS

WERE 40/50 MODELS, FOR THEIR 40 TAXABLE

HORSEPOWER AND THEIR 50 REAL HORSEPOWER.

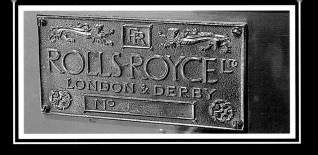

ABOVE • **The 1907 AX201 Silver Ghost has more than a million miles on the odometer. It is painted silver and the headlights and windshield trim are silver-plated.**

Claude Johnson decreed that the company should concentrate on building one model, rather than the three or four that it had been building to then. This corporate philosophy was entered into the minutes of a directors' meeting of May 13, 1908. However, the principle had been put into practice a year earlier.

While the 40/50 followed the 30-horsepower model, the two were not related that closely. For example, the engine of the Thirty was a six made up of three pairs of two cylinders cast en bloc. The 40/50 engine, on the other hand, was two blocks of three cylinders with a common crankshaft. From his earlier V-8 engine, Royce decided on a "square" design, with the bore and stroke

the same at 4.5 inches, yielding a displacement of 7.0 liters. Royce also chose a side-valve L-head configuration. All the valves were on the same side of the block and were operated by one camshaft. On the other side of the engine were the carburetor (a Royce design) and exhaust manifold. The ignition was a combined coil/battery and magneto unit built by Bosch. Each cylinder had two spark plugs.

Both the 30-horsepower and the 40/50 had rugged steel frames with six cross members and wide leaf springs for the front and rear suspensions.

Production originally began at Manchester, but moved to Derby in July 1908.

RIGHT • **In 1907, AX201 is pictured at the start of a test run with other Rolls-Royce cars.**

The first 40/50 to get a name, according to Kenneth Ullyet, author of *The Book of the Silver Ghost*, was the nineteenth chassis to be built, which was sold to Captain Guy Ward. Claude Johnson called it Grey Ghost.

By far the most famous of the 40/50 models is chassis number 60551, the twelfth chassis to be built, and license-plate number AX 201, the first Silver Ghost.

THAT'S SHOWING 'EM

Rolls-Royce first exhibited the 40/50 at the November 1906 London Motor Show in Olympia Hall. Of the two exhibits, one was a polished chassis placed atop a mirror to reveal the bottom of the engine with the oil pan removed. The other was a Barker-bodied Pullman limousine. A third car stood outside, offering demonstration rides. All the other cars on exhibit on the Rolls-Royce stand were ignored, which prompted the company to eventually discontinue production of all the other models and concentrate on the 40/50. The first customer 40/50 was delivered on April 26, 1907.

Barker & Company built a four/five-seater touring body. The body was aluminum and all the external fittings were silver-plated. On the scuttle was a silver-plated brass plate with the name "Silver Ghost."

One of the first outings for chassis 60551 was a 2,000-mile journey in May 1907, which was supervised by the Royal Automobile Club. The course followed was that of the upcoming Scottish Reliability Trials and the outing served as a reconnaissance run for that event. When the car completed the trip, the RAC took it apart and discovered only slight wear in the differential gear and piston rings.

In April 1907, the car participated in the Scottish Reliability Trials and won a gold medal. Claude Johnson received RAC approval for the car to continue after the trials in an attempt to beat the existing nonstop record. The Silver Ghost was driven around the clock on a course between London and Glasgow. The only time the engine was stopped was on Sundays, when the car was placed in a garage under scrutiny to avoid any unofficial repairs or preparation.

The Silver Ghost continued this test through August 1907. The old record was more than doubled and the Silver Ghost finished with 14,371 nonstop miles. After the trial, Claude Johnson asked the RAC officials to again take the car apart and examine the parts for wear. The total repair costs to make the car as good as new was two pounds, two shillings, and seven pence (the modern sterling equivalent is £2.13).

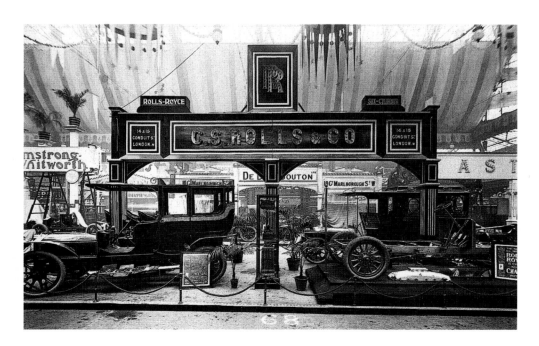

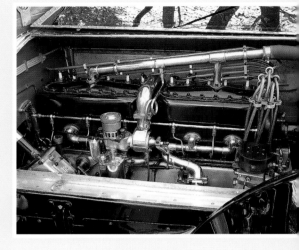

CLOCKWISE FROM TOP LEFT: The passenger compartment of the J. Rothschild & Fils Roi des Belges had a sofa-like rear seat with two jump seats for occasional passengers.

The engine of the 1907 40/50 was an inline six of 7 liters capacity. It developed an estimated 48 horsepower in 1907, but by 1925 improvements raised that to 85 hp.

Unlike the "boa constrictor" horn on AX201, the Rothschild & Fils 40/50 had four trumpet horns.

J. Rothschild & Fils built this Roi des Belges body on a 1907 40/50 Silver Ghost chassis.

WORLD CHAMPION

"At whatever speed this car is being driven on its direct third, there is no engine as far as sensation goes, nor are one's auditory nerves troubled driving or standing by a fuller sound than emanates from an eight-day clock," according to *The Autocar* in 1907. "There is no realization of driving propulsion; the feeling as the passenger sits either at the front or the back of the vehicle is one of being wafted through the landscape."

The British motoring press soon hailed the Silver Ghost as "the best car in the world."

After the Reliability Trial and the distance record, the car was sold to Dan Hanbury. He drove the car for more than 400,000 miles. In 1948, Rolls-Royce bought the car back and has put an additional 300,000 miles on the clock. It is used on special occasions and has participated in the Rose Bowl Parade and Macy's Thanksgiving Day Parade.

Rolls-Royce priced the 40/50 at $4,800 for the chassis in 1907. The company estimates that it is worth in the neighborhood of $80 million today. It is not for sale. Production eventually began in August 1908 at a rate of four cars per month.

The engine for later 40/50 models was a 7,428-cc inline six, cast as two groups of three cylinders with the bore extended to 4.75 inches. The longer stroke, however, led to crankcase vibrations at certain engine speeds. This in turn led to uneven loading of the main bearings. Royce attempted to solve the problem, but was unable to do so quickly. Vibration was cured by adding another vibration damper. This "slipper flywheel" was first mounted externally on the front of the crankshaft. Later it was moved inside the timing gear cover.

Each cylinder had dual ignition and two valves per cylinder, with cast iron pistons for lightness. One set of spark plugs ran off a trembler coil system, the other by magneto. Despite an earlier attempt at using overhead camshafts, Rolls-Royce decided in favor of side valves because they were quieter and more suitable for a luxurious and high-quality car. The head and block were cast in one piece. Power was estimated at 48 horsepower at 1,800 rpm.

Henry Royce, who was a master electrician, also designed the trembler coil. The wooden box containing the coil is mounted on the aluminum bulkhead on the passenger side. The lower half of the box is polished oak and the upper half is aluminum. On top of the removable upper half is a Rolls-Royce chassis number plate. Inside the lid is a set of instructions on the proper maintenance of the coils.

Henry Royce designed the brass carburetor for the engine. Since components of the engine itself are constructed of brass and copper, the simple Royce carburetor complements the design. "Each piece of it is pared, shaped, and arranged so," noted the artist Melbourne Brindle in *20 Silver Ghosts: The Incomparable Pre-World War I Rolls-Royce*. "Contrary to legend, Rolls-Royce did not seal the carburetor at the factory. The company did attach a plate with the following legend: 'This carburetter is accurately adjusted and should not be altered without first consulting Rolls-Royce Ltd.' "

Driving the wheels was a four-speed transmission with the shifter mounted outside, depending on the body. The gearbox itself is mounted in the center of the car rather than connected to the engine to reduce the length of the linkages. At the end of 1909 the four-speed

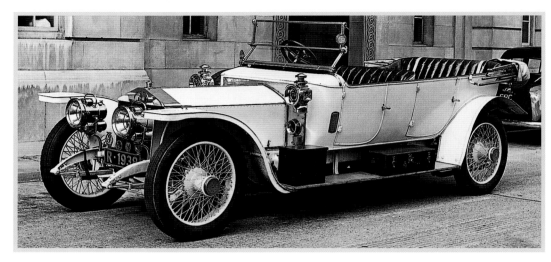

ABOVE • T.E. Lawrence, "Lawrence of Arabia," used an armored 40/50 in the desert during World War I. In his book, "Seven Pillars of Wisdom," he wrote, "A Rolls in the desert was above rubies."

ABOVE RIGHT • Rolls-Royce was able to approach perfection in its automobiles because it didn't indulge in annual model changes and left the body distinctions to the coachbuilders.

gearbox was replaced by a three-speed unit. Three gears were adequate at the time because the engine developed such great torque. In 1913 the four-speed gearbox returned, and with it a new transmission brake. Cantilevered springs, experimented with on the 1911 London–Edinburgh Tourer, became standard, along with wire wheels in 1912.

Steering is by ball and socket. There is a solid front axle with semi-elliptic leaf springs. Early Silver Ghosts used an I-beam front axle with a dropped center section. In 1909 the front axle was modified to more closely complement the radiator. The live rear axle consists of cantilevered semi-elliptic leaf springs. Rolls-Royce changed the rear suspension design several times over the course of the model's 18-year life, finally settling on cantilevered springs rather than the platform springs that were used on the early cars. There are drum brakes on the rear, none on the front.

Rolls-Royce used a combination of angular cross members, tapering side rails, and two trusses under each side rail for the frame. This arrangement could stand the harshest punishment. During World War I, Rolls-Royce armored cars carried up to four tons of armor plate, crews, and equipment, and the frame was able to hold it all without sagging or bending.

Rolls-Royce mounted the oval fuel tank on the rear of the car, unlike the other manufacturers of the time, who mounted their fuel tanks under the seats. This type of mounting made it inconvenient for passengers, who had to dismount every time fuel was added. Bronze cups that were incorporated into the mountings at each end insulated the car and tank from each other. Two tail-lamp brackets were fitted at each end of the tank, although only one was used. Rolls-Royce also mounted a reserve oil tank on the frame side rail.

Dunlop grooved, square-tread, beaded, 895 x 195 tires ride on 10-spoke wooden artillery-type wheels in front, 14-spoke wheels in the rear. Early Silver Ghosts had nondetachable rims.

Critical dimensions are a wheelbase of 143.5 inches, overall length of 192 inches, width of 62.5 inches and height of 61 inches. The Silver Ghost chassis alone weighs 2,865 pounds.

Spark and throttle controls are located in the center of the steering wheel, with a design different from all other cars of the era. The spark lever is located on the right and sets ignition timing from early to late. On the left is the throttle lever, which has the same feel as the spark lever. This lever governs the speed from fast to slow. There is a delicate lever at the top of the wheel-mounted control that regulates the fuel mixture from weak to strong. Below the carburetor lever is a knurled knob in the center of the control panel. The four positions are "B" for battery ignition, "M" for magneto ignition, "M and B" for both, and "O" for off.

SPECIAL SILVER GHOSTS

Frank Norbury of Manchester decided in 1907 it was time to introduce the Silver Ghost to India. Norbury was a retired printer, whose prime product was colored labels attached to fabrics that were sold to China and India.

He bought chassis 37 of the 40/50 model run and had it with Joseph Cockshoot bodywork. It received a portable-top limousine body in which the entire roof of the car was removable. It had a folding luggage carrier at the rear, combined with a seat for a servant. The roof rack carried a matched set of Finnigan trunks in brown leather. One of the two spare tires also had its own fitted Finnigan case while the other rode outside. Above each side window in the passenger section were ventilators for flow-through ventilation. The interior was trimmed in supple brown leather.

The car became known as the Pearl of the East. It was first exhibited at the 1908 Bombay Motor Show and won the prize for appearance. It completed a 620-mile reliability trial that included six mountain passes in the Western Ghats Mountains. No tools or spare parts were carried and the hood was locked. No unscheduled stops were needed. The car won the Mysore Cup, two gold medals, a silver cup, and two diplomas for winning the trial, and shortly after the trial, Norbury sold the car to the Maharajah of Gwailor.

After that, Rolls-Royce became the preferred car of the princes of India. The Nizam of Hyderabad reportedly owned as many as 50 at one time. Maharajah Kumer of Vizianagram ordered one for tiger shooting and the one shown below was built for the Maharajah of Alwar. The Maharajah of Patiala owned 22 Rolls-Royces and in 1921 the Nawab of Rampur ordered three identical Silver Ghosts with touring bodies by the Grosvenor Carriage Company.

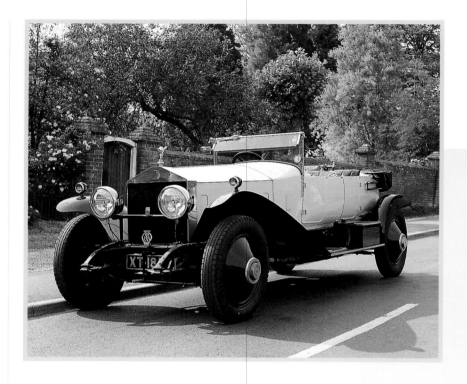

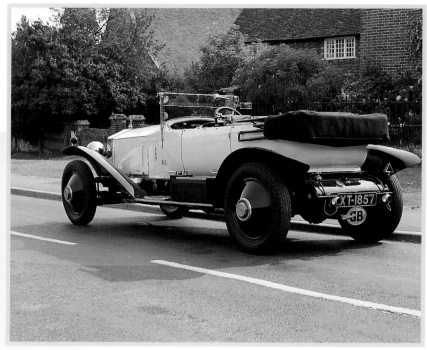

DESIGNS FOR COMFORT

On the back side of the steering wheel are deep indentations that accept the driver's fingers. The wheel is made of black material that extends halfway down the four aluminum spokes of the wheel. The steering column itself is thin. Halfway down it a small box with a bearing and an oil cup is attached. Farther down the column on touring cars is a tubular brace to strengthen the column. On enclosed cars there is a shorter column, which is bolted to the bulkhead for support. At the base of the column is the steering box, made of cast aluminum with the Rolls-Royce emblem on it.

Of course no Rolls-Royce would be a Rolls-Royce without the famous radiator grille. The classic radiator first appeared on 1904 cars. It was so simple and perfect that it is one of the few radiator grilles to survive 90-plus years. On the Silver Ghost, the radiator is mounted above the axle.

Just before World War I the car earned an electric starter, electric

ABOVE LEFT • **This 1924 40/50 Silver Ghost Tourer by T.H. Gill had a yellow primrose body and black fenders.**

ABOVE RIGHT • **The T.H. Gill 1924 Tourer was one of the first to incorporate four-wheel brakes, introduced in 1923.**

BELOW • **One of the more interesting Silver Ghost variations is this 1920 40/50 four-door eight-window sedan with an aerodynamic rear.**

lighting, and forged steel connecting rods. Light alloy pistons were introduced during the war.

Four-wheel brakes were finally installed after November 1923. One of the reasons may have been criticism of the brakes by *The Motor* in one of its first road tests in 1919. The magazine was able to achieve a top speed of 78 mph in its test car. But there was criticism of the brakes. While they worked well enough, the task of stopping a two-ton car with four adults in it from a speed of 78 mph with a transmission brake and two rear drum brakes was daunting. Rolls-Royce recognized the possible safety problem and began installing four-wheel brakes after December 1923. The four-wheel brakes were mechanically actuated and had a mechanical power assist.

The last Silver Ghost ordered was on December 19, 1924. It was sold to a man who already owned a 1909 Silver Ghost that had served him well for more than 300,000 miles. The car had a Barker tourer body and was delivered on June 3, 1925.

Rarely in history has a mistress—or "companion"—been so honored. But Miss Eleanor Thornton, because of her employment as private secretary to one of the world's first automobile enthusiasts—as well as her employment as secretary and her friendship with one of the artists of the magazine with which they both were associated—has forever earned the sobriquet, "Spirit of Ecstasy."

Lord John Scott-Montagu of Beaulieu (pronounced "Bewly") was the first British driver, with Charles Rolls, to race on the Continent in the 1899 Paris–Ostend. A consummate automobile enthusiast, he sponsored a bill in Parliament that legalized the first auto race in Great Britain, the Irish Gordon Bennett Cup race of 1903. He also sponsored a bill that created license plates in Britain, not one of his more popular acts.

Montagu was at the opening of the Rolls-Royce plant in Derby in July 1908, and owned Rolls-Royces from that day onward. In fact, when a neighbor tried to convince him of the benefits of his new Leyland Eight, Montagu would have nothing to do with it.

Montagu also founded the magazine *Car Illustrated* in 1902. This was an upscale magazine devoted to the automobile. He was a prolific author who penned several books on automobiles. His son has also authored books on such marques as Jaguar and, naturally, Rolls-Royce.

The staff artist on the magazine was Charles Sykes, whose well-known caricatures in *Car Illustrated* satirized those in the British public who were anti-automobile.

Sykes also had a reputation as a sculptor. He was a graduate of London's Royal College of Art, and his work included the Montagu Trophy, awarded to the team in the 1903 Gordon Bennett Cup race for the best overall performance. The figure topping the trophy has a strong resemblance to Montagu's secretary, Eleanor Thornton, although there are few solid foundations to the rumors surrounding their relationship. Montagu's son, the second Lord Montagu of Beaulieu, admitted in an interview reported in *Automobile Quarterly* that Miss Thornton was "very much more than a secretary, but...she acted with consummate dignity."

Sykes also sculpted hood ornaments for some of Montagu's cars, gracing the radiators of the lord's cars with unique sculptures. Unlike today, when only a few distinct marques have protruding hood ornaments, almost all vehicles had some ornamentation in the early years of the century. The ubiquitous motometer, for example, was the most popular, providing an idea of radiator coolant temperature. In Britain, a popular ornament was a buffoon policeman—one way of getting back at those officers who might harass drivers.

Montagu commissioned Sykes to design "Whisper"—a hood ornament that depicted a woman in a flowing gown with one finger pressed to her lips, reflecting the sculpture's name. It would be on every Rolls-Royce that Montagu owned.

ABOVE • **The modern Spirit of Ecstasy is three inches tall and is spring-loaded to retract into the radiator shell if it is struck from any direction.**

ABOVE • **The Spirit of Ecstasy has changed over the years from its original form on the far right, through the kneeling version, to the slightly smaller version in use today on the far left.**

Claude Johnson had been looking for a suitable radiator ornament for the Silver Ghost. When he saw Sykes's sketches for "Whisper" he suggested that the model would make an excellent figurehead for the Silver Ghost. Johnson asked Sykes to evoke something of the spirit of the mythical beauty Nike, whose sculpted image was in the Louvre, Paris. Sykes opted for a more feminine and graceful representation.

At the instigation of Montagu, Sykes designed the "Spirit of Ecstasy" for Rolls-Royce cars. In Sykes's words, reported in *Automobile Quarterly*, the Spirit of Ecstasy was a girl "who has selected road travel as her supreme delight and has alighted on the prow of a Rolls-Royce car to revel in the freshness of the air and the musical sound of her fluttering draperies." These "draperies" consisted of a diaphanous gown flowing tight against the model's body with her arms spread backward, simulating wings.

Rolls-Royce offered the "figureheads" beginning in 1911 at a modest cost. She was first cast as a standing woman, leaning slightly forward. The statuette was originally 5.75 inches tall. By 1912 it had become standard equipment from the factory. In 1933, Sykes was commissioned to modernize the Spirit of Ecstasy.

He changed the sculpture slightly by putting the Spirit of Ecstasy in a kneeling position, but she was still leaning forward into the wind. This kneeling version was said by the company to afford better vision for a more sporting type of body.

Since 1948, the Spirit of Ecstasy has been cast in stainless steel, while previous versions were made of nickel and bronze. And, despite the legend, it has never been cast in solid silver by the factory. In the 1960s, the Spirit returned to a standing position, but it was produced slightly smaller at 4.25 inches.

Today's Spirit of Ecstasy stands three inches tall. For safety, she is mounted to a spring-loaded mechanism that is designed to retract into the radiator shell if she is struck from any direction.

The American author Ken Purdy (*The Kings of the Road*) tells of certain Rolls-Royce owners who, "on parking the car for any extended period, always remove [the Spirit of Ecstasy] and replace it with the thoughtfully provided plain cap." Purdy also notes that the Royal Phantoms have, instead of the Spirit, a statuette of St George slaying the dragon. Purdy wrote,

"When the builders of the car first saw the piece they found it quite acceptable as art but wanting in

LEFT • Each Spirit of Ecstasy is formed in wax and hand-finished with a hot scalpel. It is then sprayed with a ceramic material, the wax melted out and replaced with molten stainless steel.

TOP • The original Spirit was believed to be modeled on Miss Eleanor Thornton, secretary to Lord John Scott Montagu of Beaulieu.

ABOVE • The modern Spirit is produced to be smaller and more dainty than the original.

engineering. They wondered if the mass of horse and rider, highly placed as it was, might not eventually detach itself from the dragon, writhing below. A suitable testing machine was devised and the statue was bumped and banged in a way that a year of riding over railroad tracks could not duplicate. As a result the statue was redesigned with a view to better apportioning of the stresses. The dragon's head was moved to support the horse from the side, and the dragon's tongue was imperceptibly lengthened in order to furnish support for the horse's belly, while St. George's lance was firmly imbedded in the evil beast, the better to support the rider. As art, the statue is still good; as engineering, it now meets Rolls-Royce standards and thus can never, never be jounced the least bit out of line!"

Unfortunately, Miss Thornton never lived to enjoy her fame as the model for the Spirit of Ecstasy. She traveled with Lord Montagu to India where he served as Inspector of Mechanical Transport. On their return to London in December 1915 their ship was torpedoed off the island of Crete and sank. Lord Montagu was among only 11 survivors of the sinking. He was blown to the surface by an underwater explosion. Miss Thornton, however, was not as lucky.

THE COACHBUILT YEARS

CLOCKWISE FROM TOP:
Detail of the rear wheel arch hood of the 1933 20/25 Rolls-Royce Landaulette by Hooper.

The rear mudguard of a 1937 Gurney Nutting 25/30 convertible.

Headlights and grille of the 1947 Silver Wraith Sedanca that Hooper built for oil billionaire Nubar Gulbenkian.

Barker, who built most of the early Rolls-Royce bodies, built this Sports Saloon body on a 1930 20/25 chassis.

COACHBUILDERS HAVE LONG HAD A GOOD RELATIONSHIP WITH ROLLS-ROYCE. FROM THE BEGINNING, ROLLS-ROYCE SOLD ONLY CHASSIS, AND LEFT IT TO THE BUYERS TO HAVE BODIES BUILT ON THOSE CHASSIS. OCCASIONALLY, THE COMPANY WOULD MAKE AVAILABLE A BARKER-BUILT BODY ON SOME OF THE EARLIER CHASSIS, BUT IN GENERAL IT WAS LEFT TO THE BUYER TO CHOOSE. SOME OF THESE BODY DESIGNS HAVE GONE DOWN IN HISTORY AS THE MOST EXQUISITE AUTOMOBILES EVER CONSTRUCTED. OTHERS, PERHAPS, ARE BEST FORGOTTEN. IN ANY CASE, THE COMPANIES THAT DESIGNED AND BUILT BODIES FOR ROLLS-ROYCES HAVE BEEN AMONG THE MOST PRESTIGIOUS BODY BUILDERS IN THE WORLD.

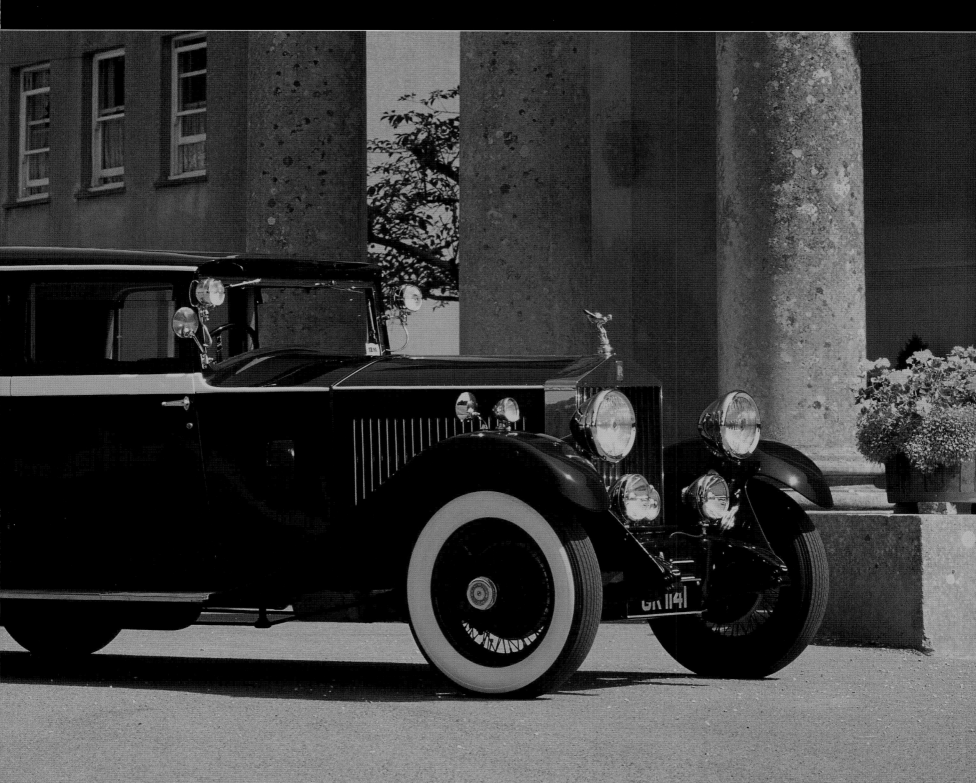

ABOVE • **Barker built many barrel-sided tourers on 20 hp chassis. This 1924 version displays the horizontal grillework peculiar to the 20 hp.**

When Rolls-Royce changed from the separate-chassis-and-body style of construction to unibody or mono-coque, it was forced into the business of bodybuilding as well as chassis construction. However, the firm of Mulliner Park Ward had become an in-house coach-builder, so little of the flair of the past was lost, except that now all Rolls-Royces (and Bentleys) looked alike.

The first of these coachbuilders, as we have said, was Barker. The first Rolls-Royce 10-horsepower cars were available with two- or four-passenger bodies built by Barker & Co. of London. Barker was also the coachbuilder of choice for the 1905 20-horsepower

model. According to Halwart Schrader in *Rolls-Royce Cars and Bentley from 1931*,

"Carriage-making practices still prevailed and windshields were an option. Front seats were mounted higher, as for a coachman on a horse-drawn vehicle. The brougham with its closed cabin for the passengers and a cover for the driver was an exception. Most touring cars were fitted with open phaeton bodies, offering seating sometimes for two, but usually four or six people."

The first Rolls-Royce grille, modeled after a Greek temple. In more than 95 years of production, the essential shape has remained.

LEFT • In 1923, Barker also built this open-drive Limousine body on a 20 hp chassis.

BELOW • This 1926 20 hp Cabriolet de Ville with coachwork by Barker exhibits "wood grain" metalwork. The 20 hp was intended as a "small car" to complement the 40/50 Silver Ghost.

RIGHT • Barker and Company was the premier coachbuilder on early Rolls-Royce chassis. This 1930 20/25 Continental Sports Sedan is a particularly fine example of their work a quarter century later.

FAR RIGHT TOP • With the extended boot (trunk), it wasn't necessary to compromise rear seating for intruding luggage.

FAR RIGHT MIDDLE • Right-hand drive (of course) and center-mounted instruments are interior details of the Barker Continental Sports Sedan. Note the open fresh-air door at the driver's feet; an example of early air conditioning.

FAR RIGHT BOTTOM • The front of the Barker 20/25 Continental Sports Sedan featured large 'bullet' headlamps, matching fog lamps, and the classic Grecian temple-inspired Rolls-Royce grille.

ABOVE • **This 1937 25/30 Barker Rolls-Royce Sports Sedan is externally similar to the 1930 car pictured previously. The only difference was that the 3.7-liter inline six of the earlier car was enlarged to 4.26 liters and the estimated horsepower increased from 100 to 115.**

When they were first approached to build bodies for Rolls-Royce automobiles, Barker had been building royal coaches since 1710 and had built up a fine reputation. Many of the classic coachbuilding firms, in both Europe and the United States, got their start building horse-drawn coaches. The tradition, building approach, and style of the vehicles quite naturally followed those of the horse-drawn coaches, giving credence to the name "horseless carriages."

Barker continued building bodies into the 1930s. An order book that was growing smaller forced a merger with Hooper & Co. in 1938. But, in the time Barker built Rolls-Royce bodies, they built them for regular customers as well as royalty. One of their earliest was a phaeton in Roi des Belges style, but they also built limousines, tourers, and cabriolets. Schrader calls the Sedanca de Ville "a specialty of the house."

Hooper, which came into existence in 1807 and began building bodies on Rolls-Royce chassis in 1909, was among the most experimental of coachbuilders in England. Hooper has built car and coach bodies for Queen Elizabeth II and five of her predecessors, beginning with Queen Victoria.

Hooper built its first car body for royalty in 1899, a decade before working with Rolls-Royce. The car was for the future King Edward VII and its body was built on a six-horsepower Daimler chassis. By 1910, the company was making limousine bodies for King George V. Hooper's first Rolls-Royce body was made in 1909 on a Silver Ghost chassis. David Owen, writing in *Automobile Quarterly*, noted, "In many ways, this was more significant than the King's carriages, since the Ghost best suited the type of customer who could appreciate, and afford, Hooper's craftsmanship. One typical Ghost

TOP LEFT • The doors of the Hooper Limousine were hinged at the front and back, providing easy entry. Note the substantial side support on the adjustable front bucket seats.

TOP RIGHT • The Hooper 20 hp Limousine had an aerodynamic rear end and a side-mounted spare.

LEFT • Hooper built this limousine body on a 1927 20 hp Rolls-Royce chassis. The car featured adjustable front bucket seats, a crash gearbox, tilted steering column, and twin tool boxes.

BOTTOM LEFT • Detail of the bulb horn on the windshield pillar.

BOTTOM MIDDLE • Only a chrome klaxon horn would be adequate for a Hooper-bodied 1927 20 hp Rolls-Royce Limousine.

BOTTOM RIGHT • The dash of the 1927 20 hp Hooper-bodied Rolls-Royce Limousine (opposite) has instruments centered in front of the driver and to the left in burl walnut.

owner was the writer Rudyard Kipling, author of *The Jungle Book*, who had a Roi des Belges body built by Hooper on his 1913 Silver Ghost."

At the 1920 London Motor Show, Hooper displayed a Rolls-Royce Silver Ghost landaulette-limousine. This car was a combination of a closed sedan and a convertible. It had openings in the front and rear for the chauffeur and passengers as well as a divider in the middle. Rolls-Royce also exhibited a Hooper-bodied Silver Ghost on its stand. This car was a four-seater tourer with a yellow body and black fenders and trim. The upholstery was red leather. Wheel discs covered the wire wheels.

While this Silver Ghost may have been the first, it was not the last of Hooper's designs that were considered avant garde. Earning that honor, at least on Rolls-Royce chassis (Hooper made several trademark ugly cars on Daimler chassis for Sir Bernard Docker and his wife), was an aerodynamic, enclosed body on a 1947 Silver Wraith chassis for the oil billionaire Nubar Gulbenkian.

The Gulbenkian Silver Wraith was a Sedanca de Ville body with fully enclosed front and rear wheels. The body enveloped the entire car and dipped to within inches of the road surface. Because of the enclosed wheels, the car was nearly seven feet wide in order to permit the front wheels to turn without hitting the fenders. The sides were flat, including recessed door handles.

Even the famous Rolls-Royce radiator was disguised with a curved horizontal-slatted copy that may have

A TIMELY WARNING...

At the end of the nineteenth century, Hooper & Co. produced an advertising booklet for its potential customers. In it, the company warned,

"Strangely enough many people who would not entrust a 5-guinea watch to any but a maker of repute, will send, or permit to be sent, a 150-guinea carriage to the nearest individual who may have rented a stable in some mews and called himself a 'coachbuilder.' We recommend finding an old-established coachbuilder which had made carriages for Royalty and 'distinguished personages' and had won prizes 'in competition with other firms at some of the great International Exhibitions.'"

been more aerodynamic but certainly wasn't Rolls-Royce.
A horizontal grillework also covered the headlights and
smaller driving lights.

Hooper painted the car in two-tone bronze.
Upholstery was dark-brown leather in front and two-
tones West of England cloth in the rear. The Hooper
woodwork inside was painted to match the exterior.
David Owen noted, "It looked about as distinguished
and imposing as a grown-up Austin Atlantic, though a
wealthy private customer, with the funds to back his
own ideas, however bizarre, was still a welcome stranger
in the late Forties."

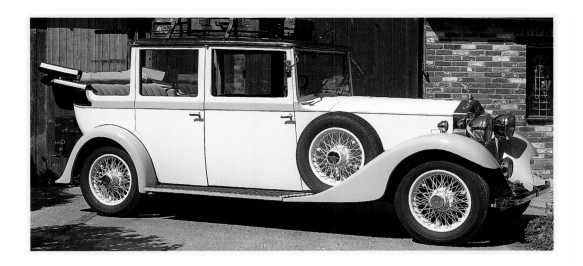

CLOCKWISE FROM TOP: **This
1933 20/25 Rolls-Royce Landaulette
by Hooper was named for its
convertible rear section.**

**With its top up, it resembled any
other 20/25 Rolls-Royce sedan.**

**Under the hood was a 3669cc inline
six rated at about 100 horsepower.**

**As with the dash of the 1930 Barker
20/25 Rolls-Royce, the instruments of
were center-mounted.**

**The rear seat of the Hooper 20/25
Landaulette was a comfortable couch
with spacious legroom.**

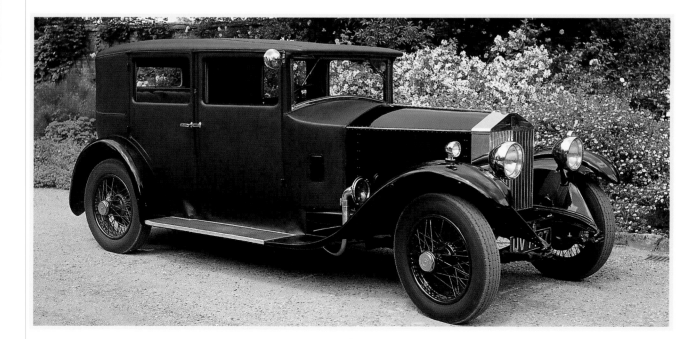

HOOPER ON SHOW

The 1924 London Auto Show saw the Hooper stand display a 40/50-horsepower Rolls-Royce with a closed cabriolet body in two-tone gray, with the upholstery in gray cloth and calfskin. The woodwork was burr walnut inlaid with ebony and onyx. Hooper also added a small bar that had a disappearing cover similar to a roll-top desk turned sideways.

Hooper displayed a Phantom I enclosed cabriolet at the 1926 show that had a removable panel over the driver that could be slid back if the driver wanted fresh air. Back in the passenger compartment was a heater that was warmed by the car's exhaust and used battery-powered lamps to simulate glowing coals. The upholstery was blue horsehair cloth and the wood was quartered laurel.

A landscape painter named Michaelis had a Hooper-bodied Phantom II that was equipped as a mobile studio, complete with an opening roof that could be converted into an easel.

When Rolls-Royce created the Phantom IV for royalty and heads of state, it built only 17 examples. Six of these had bodies by Hooper. Among these were a Sedanca de Ville for the Aga Khan, two touring limousines for King Feisal of Iraq and his brother, a landaulette for Queen Elizabeth II, a seven-passenger limousine for Princess Marina, and a black limousine for the Shah of Iran.

This last car was a bone of contention between the Shah's family and his successors. When the Ayatollah Khomeini took control of Iran, the Rolls-Royce was back in London for a major overhaul, including a new engine. This car, and a Silver Ghost which was also being repaired, was claimed by both the Shah's family and the new government, which claimed it had been paid for by the Iranian people. Rolls-Royce decided to leave the decision to the lawyers, who decided in favor of the Ayatollah.

The Aga Khan's similar vehicle had mirrors on the inside of the rear windows and a leather-lined tray in the folding center-rear armrest that contained a comb, clothes brush, two cut-glass jars with silver tops, and a solid-silver powder compact. Between the two folding seats was a polished-wood cabinet with two thermos flasks, two sandwich boxes, four plates, and four nested silver cups, as well as two small picnic tables.

When the market for coachbuilt cars of extreme luxury dried up, so did Hooper's fortunes. Its factory closed in 1960 when it was a subsidiary of BSA, which also controlled Daimler. There is a new Hooper with no connection to the former company. This company does conversions on Rolls-Royce and Bentley cars.

Park Ward shared a relationship with Rolls-Royce similar to that of the Fisher Brothers with General Motors. Park Ward was established in 1919 and was eventually absorbed by Rolls-Royce 20 years later, when as much as 95 percent of its production was for the company. The Park Ward name has been retained as a trademark for Rolls-Royce's own coachbuilding department within the company.

Park Ward also built convertibles and coupes on the R-Type Bentley Continental chassis. When the Silver Cloud was offered in a 127-inch wheelbase instead of the original 124-inch, Park Ward modified the steel sedans to include an extra four inches in the rear passenger compartment. The company was also credited with a slab-sided drophead coupe built on the Silver Cloud II chassis.

ABOVE • **The 1937 Gurney Nutting 20/25 convertible featured enclosed rear wheels and a long sloping tail with an inset spare tire.**

RIGHT • **This 1937 25/30 Rolls-Royce with a convertible body by Gurney Nutting shows the advances in aerodynamics developed in the 1930s.**

The other formerly independent coachbuilder that became a part of Rolls-Royce was H. J. Mulliner, established in 1900. This happened in 1961, when Mulliner was faced with that choice or bankruptcy. Again, as with the Fishers and GM, Mulliner Park Ward is the in-house coachbuilding firm of Rolls-Royce.

H. J. Mulliner was one of several coachbuilders who used the Weymann method of construction. In the simplest terms, this involved framing the body in ash wood in order to avoid squeaks, then applying a leathercloth body to the framing.

Mulliner bodies on the 25/30, for example, incorporated an enclosed luggage compartment, unlike many contemporary coachbuilders, who simply bolted a trunk of some sort to the rear of the car. These compartments could be accessed through small doors. These were also usually fitted with optional luggage carriers, which were folding racks mounted near the rear bumpers. Suitcases could be strapped to these racks.

James Young was an independent coachbuilder with a flair for experimenting with design, building a fastback sports sedan on a 1935 20/25 chassis, as well as a particularly handsome cabriolet on the same chassis. In 1933, James Young built a Sedanca de Ville body on a Phantom II chassis with decorative landau irons. This two-toned vehicle featured an open driver's compartment and closed passenger compartment.

James Young was noted as being an early convert to front-hinged doors at a time when other coachbuilders were putting hinges on doors in every possible location: both opening to the front, both hinged in the center, both opening in the center. James Young used cantilevered sliding doors on a 1938 Phantom III, for example, showing that no coachbuilder was firmly attached to one design.

Gurney Nutting was noted for bodies on the Phantom II that included a four-door sedan and a drophead coupe.

Most of these elegant bodies were built on a succession of Rolls-Royce chassis that followed the Silver Ghost. The first among these was the 20-horsepower, manufactured between 1922 and 1929. The 20-horsepower, which is often referred to as the "Baby Rolls," was developed more for owner-drivers. It was smaller than the Silver Ghost, and therefore didn't require the attention of a chauffeur. For example, the Silver Ghost had 99 grease points that had to be serviced weekly. It was more than 16 feet long and weighed more than two tons, making driving it in city streets more the job of a professional than an owner.

Besides, American manufacturers such as Cadillac, Stutz, Reo, and Franklin, not to mention Ford, were building good cars that their owners could drive themselves. There was still a market for the executive car for upper-class gentlemen, but Rolls-Royce decided it was interested in meeting the needs of a slightly different market.

SPECTER ON THE SANDS

One particular Park Ward body deserves special mention. This was a Phantom III with a heavy limousine body, which was tested in an African run. The Phantom completed the 2,200-mile run from Algeria to Kano, Nigeria in three days, 7½ hours, including a stretch across the Sahara Desert. The temperature inside the car at times reached 188 degrees. H. E. Symons, who was on the ride, said that the entire journey totaled 12,500 miles, including the trip from England to Nairobi, Kenya, and back. No water was added to the radiator and the springs remained intact, despite having to traverse the desert and every other kind of African road surface.

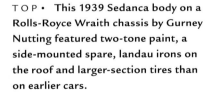

TOP • **This 1939 Sedanca body on a Rolls-Royce Wraith chassis by Gurney Nutting featured two-tone paint, a side-mounted spare, landau irons on the roof and larger-section tires than on earlier cars.**

MIDDLE • **Thrupp & Maberly built this Sedanca de Ville on a 1929 Rolls-Royce 20 hp chassis.**

BOTTOM • **Five years later, Thrupp & Maberly built this Convertible body on a 25/30 Rolls-Royce chassis. Note the improvements in aerodynamics from the car above.**

RIGHT • The Rolls-Royce
20 hp chassis is instantly
identifiable by the adjustable
horizontal radiator slats. This
was a one-model experiment
that was never tried again.

BELOW • This Rolls-Royce
1926 Doctor's Coupe on a
20 hp chassis was built by
William Arnold of Manchester.
It exhibits narrow-section tires
on wire wheels and a lone
enclosed trunk.

WITH SAFETY IN MIND

Since the 20-horsepower and its successors probably
wouldn't receive the attention and upkeep from their
owner-drivers that the Silver Ghost would enjoy, the
company built in safeguards to protect it from this
reduced maintenance schedule.

Built on a 120-inch wheelbase, the 20-horsepower was
introduced in September 1922. The engine was a 3.1-liter
six, which produced an estimated 80 horsepower. This
was the first Rolls-Royce engine with a detachable
cylinder head and a one-piece cylinder block. It
incorporated overhead valves and a camshaft mounted
in the side of the block. Only one spark plug per
cylinder was used.

Initially, the gearbox was a three-speed affair, but in
1925 an extra gear was added. With either gearbox, it was

possible to run as low as 10 mph in top gear and then accelerate up to 60 mph with no problems. The three-speed box offered a centrally mounted gearshift, but with the four-speed the gearshift was moved to the right in conjunction with the handbrake.

The 20-horsepower was instantly recognizable from the front. It shared the same "Grecian temple" grille of the Silver Ghost, but the "columns" were now horizontal. These adjustable shutters controlled the engine temperature, but immediately classified the 20-horsepower as a "different" Rolls-Royce. The shutters became vertical toward the end of the model's run.

While the car was marketed simply as the Twenty, the prototype had been called Cinderella and the name of Goshawk had been proposed for the car. Since a G preceded all chassis numbers, perhaps the Goshawk name remained at least in the hearts of the company.

Following the Twenty in the company's history was the New Phantom, covered in Chapter 6. The more normal "production" Rolls-Royce was the 20/25, introduced in 1929 and manufactured until 1936, during

which time 3,827 were built. The 20/25 used the same engine as the Twenty, bored out to 3.7 liters. It used the same seven-bearing crankshaft and a 4.6:1 compression ratio that resulted in an estimated 100 horsepower. As with the Twenty, a 129-inch wheelbase was used for the chassis, but this was increased to 132 inches in 1930.

Unlike the Twenty, though, the 20/25 had vertical shutters on the grille, returning to standard Rolls-Royce practice. There was a warning light on the dash that alerted the driver that the coolant temperature had reached 90 °C. In 1932, the shutters were thermostatically controlled, removing this responsibility from the driver.

All the grease points became attached to the central lubrication system in 1932 as well, making that point of maintenance easier. In 1934, a built-in jacking system was added. Center-lock wire wheels were standard, but many owners added disc wheel overlays.

Following the 20/25 was the 25/30 of 1936–38. The cylinders were bored out again, increasing displacement to 4,257 cc and output to around 115 horsepower. Top

TOP • **This Sedanca de Ville body by Windovers on a 1931 20/25 Rolls-Royce chassis exhibits a side-mounted spare, vertical side louvers on the hood, and a windshield that would raise to permit fresh air into the cabin.**

ABOVE • **Detail of the vanity set in the back of a 1931 Windovers-bodied 20/25 Sedanca de Ville.**

LEFT • This 1933 Schutter & van Bakel 20/25 close-coupled sedan is a one-of-a-kind car, built for a customer who wanted Voisin styling on a Rolls-Royce chassis.

BOTTOM LEFT • Chapron built this coupe on a 1935 20/25 Rolls-Royce chassis giving the classic Rolls-Royce sleek lines. Note the disc wheels that were beginning to replace wire wheels.

FAR LEFT • **This 1936 25/30 Rolls-Royce Landaulette by Windovers exhibits the convertible rear section typical of the Landaulette body style.**

LEFT • **Rolls-Royce introduced the Wraith in 1938, with an inline six-cylinder engine. The Wraith succeeded the 25/30.**

POWERING UP

The 4,257-cc Wraith engine, as well as its predecessors, was derived from the original 3.1-liter engine of the Twenty. To obtain more power, the bore was increased from the original 3 inches to 3.5 inches. Enough space had been designed into the engine between the cylinders to accommodate larger bores. But, as the need for more power increased, the valves were made larger, which resulted in a reduction of the cooling space between the cylinders. This led to a change in the valving arrangement that was found in cars built after World War II.

speed was on the order of 75–80 mph, depending on the body chosen.

Changes to the engine included the use of a Stromberg carburetor in place of the Rolls-Royce unit. Magneto ignition was replaced by a second coil-ignition setup, but only one operated at a time. Two SU fuel pumps replaced the Autovac system for supplying fuel to the engine. The standard wheelbase was 132 inches.

Like the previous models in the "small" Rolls-Royce line, the 25/30 used a leaf-spring suspension. It added hydraulic shock absorbers that were adjustable from the driver's seat. Ride quality was said to be better than in the Phantom I. Only 1201 25/30 chassis were produced.

The last prewar non-Phantom Rolls-Royce was the Wraith, built in 1938 and 1939. Only 491 were manufactured before war broke out and Rolls-Royce turned its interest to aircraft-engine manufacture.

Its chief engineer, A. G. Elliot, had hoped that the X-braced chassis of the Wraith would have been used on the 25/30 in 1936, rather than waiting two years. Drilling holes in nonstressed areas of the side members and X-beams lightened the frame. Rivets were used for some of the joints, as opposed to the welded joints used on the Phantom III. The Wraith also incorporated an independent front suspension, also lifted from the PIII.

While the Wraith chassis may have been originally intended for a straight-eight or V-8 engine, in the end it was the 4,257 cc unit of the 25/30 and Bentley 4¼-liter that was chosen. Modifications to the engine included a new cylinder head, different manifolding and timing gears, and larger-diameter valves. The engine (see box) developed 105 horsepower in Rolls-Royce trim.

Built on a 136-inch wheelbase chassis, the Wraith also used adjustable shock absorbers and a built-in jacking system, as in the PIII. Custom bodies were of course available, but customers were urged to buy the "standard" body produced by Park Ward, which was now a Rolls-Royce subsidiary. The two bodies available were a four-door sedan with a sunroof and a Special Saloon, which included a heater and better interior.

CLOCKWISE FROM TOP:
Detail showing the wire wheels of the Piccadilly Roadster.

Switchbox of Charlie Chaplin's 1931 Rolls-Royce Phantom II Brewster-bodied convertible.

Steering wheel detail of the Pall Mall Tourer.

Rolls-Royce began building Silver Ghosts in Springfield, Massachusetts in 1921. Merrimac had originally built this Piccadilly Roadster as a Limousine Brougham.

IT DIDN'T TAKE LONG AFTER THE CONCLUSION OF WORLD WAR I FOR THE FIRST POSTWAR ROLLS-ROYCE TO REACH THE UNITED STATES. THAT CAR WAS ALLEGEDLY DELIVERED ON OCTOBER 4, 1919. IT TOOK EVEN LESS TIME—TWO MONTHS—FOR THE ANNOUNCEMENT THAT ROLLS-ROYCE CARS WOULD BE BUILT IN THE UNITED STATES. THE NEWLY FORMED ROLLS-ROYCE OF AMERICA INC. HAD PURCHASED THE PLANT OF THE FORMER AMERICAN WIRE WHEEL COMPANY IN SPRINGFIELD, MASS., AND WOULD CONVERT THAT PLANT TO BUILD ROLLS-ROYCE CARS. ROLLS-ROYCE OF AMERICA WAS INCORPORATED WITH CAPITAL STOCK OF $7.5 MILLION ON OCTOBER 18, 1919. THE DECISION TO EXPORT PRODUCTION WAS FORCED BY A TWO-TO THREE-YEAR BACKLOG IN ORDERS IN ENGLAND.

CHASSIS PLANT – ROLLS-ROYCE OF AMERICA, INC.
Hendee Street, Springfield, Mass.

ABOVE • **American Rolls-Royces were built in this new factory in Springfield, Massachusetts, under the supervision of Maurice Olley.**

RIGHT TOP • **The interior of the Brewster Pickwick sedan shows a soft couch-like rear bench seat with foot rests.**

RIGHT BOTTOM • **Brewster built most of the bodies on Springfield Rolls-Royce 40/50 chassis. From the rear, the Pickwick sedan exhibits the rectangular styling typical of 1921.**

FAR RIGHT • **Of the 1701 40/50 Rolls-Royce chassis built in Springfield was this Brewster-bodied Pickwick sedan.**

Rolls-Royce cautioned, however, that the Springfield Rolls-Royces would be built by "British mechanics under British supervision," just to allay any fears that the American Rolls-Royces would be produced with any less attention to quality than their British counterparts. The factory was capable of building 300 to 400 cars a year with many of the machine tools brought over from England. With a new, modern factory, the setup was actually better than in England. The Springfield plant may rightfully be considered the first "transplant" factory and the factory itself one of the first "greenfield" factories. Unlike the modern Japanese and German counterparts, though, the cars were actually manufactured in Springfield, not merely "assembled."

Springfield workers were under the supervision of Maurice Olley, who had been a member of Henry Royce's design team. Five years after he moved to Derby in 1912 he was Royce's personal assistant. Like Royce, Olley was a perfectionist, and the ideal person to head up the Springfield works, he later worked for Cadillac.

The Americanization of Rolls-Royce actually had its start much earlier when Charles Rolls brought his winning TT car to the United States in December 1906. Rolls used the car in a local race, which he won. The notoriety spurred US sales of the car, but they were slow.

The first Springfield car rolled off the assembly line on January 17 (or April 28, the precise date is unknown), 1921. It was a Silver Ghost with a 143.5-inch wheelbase and a six-cylinder engine. Priced at $11,750 for the chassis, it was slightly less expensive than the British version of the same car. The car was fitted with a Merrimac body and delivered to Wallace Porter, one of the toolmakers who had helped equip the new factory.

Every chassis that came off the assembly line underwent lengthy dynamometer tests before having the body installed. It also underwent a 100- to 150-mile road test. Engines were tested at wide-open throttle for two hours. After the body was installed, the cars underwent another 300- to 350-mile road test before the buyer even saw it.

American Rolls-Royces were offered in both chassis and bodied forms. The 1922 catalog offered 11 different body styles. Custom coachbuilders such as Merrimac, Brewster, Judkins, Murphy, and Locke offered bodies. But Americans are Americans and generally preferred dealing with just one company for both the chassis and body for their cars.

When Rolls-Royce of America purchased the Brewster coachbuilding company in December 1925, it had an in-house coachbuilder whose work was of the same quality as the chassis the bodies were being placed on. Unfortunately, Rolls-Royce also inherited Brewster's debt of about $1.5 million and antiquated production facilities. Production was only 350 bodies a year. The majority of the factory was left unused, while the workers operated in cramped quarters struggling to build even that many cars.

Springfield Rolls-Royces never had four-wheel brakes because the cost of retooling would have been too expensive. Despite the high cost of the car, Springfield kept losing money. Sales never approached the goals.

Sales in 1921 were 135 cars, followed by 230 in 1922, 292 in 1924, and 359 in 1925. This was the sales goal. Prices had also been reduced over that time to make the car more competitive, but the combination didn't help the bottom line. The price in March 1924 for a Silver Ghost with a complete four-passenger Pall Mall touring car body was $10,900, sans bumpers.

RIGHT • The Piccadilly Roadster had hydraulic shock-protected tubular bumpers and a rear rumble seat.

BELOW • Originally fitted with a Limousine Brougham body, this 1923 Rolls-Royce Silver Ghost Piccadilly Roadster was rebodied in the late 1920s by Merrimac, a company that was subcontracting to Brewster.

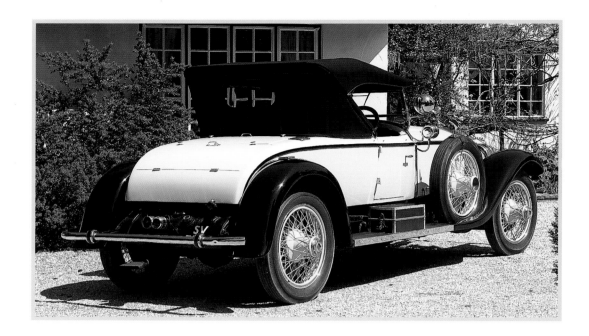

ABOVE • **This 1922 Springfield 40/50 chassis was made in Derby, England and disappeared for 35 years. When it was discovered it was without coachwork, so Brewster built this Pall Mall Tourer body for it.**

FAR LEFT • **The dash of the Pall Mall Tourer shows the instruments arrayed horizontally. The odometer reads very low mileage because of the 35 years in storage.**

LEFT • **The luggage trunk at the rear of the Pall Mall Tourer carried fitted suitcases.**

RIGHT • After Rolls-Royce began building the New Phantom in England, the Springfield factory began building left-hand-drive versions in 1931. This shift may have led to the closing of the factory.

FROM RIGHT TO LEFT

Beginning in February 1925, Springfield Rolls-Royces were produced as left-hand drive cars. The Brewster plant accepted right-hand-drive cars as trade-ins, overhauled them and rebodied them, often as two-seater roadsters. None were converted to left-hand drive, however. Many buyers of the time said they felt a left-hand-drive Rolls-Royce wasn't a true Rolls-Royce and only about 600 were made in all.

The Springfield Silver Ghost was built from 1921 to 1926. The engine was the same as the British Silver Ghost: a six-cylinder inline made up of two groups of three cylinders. The 7.4-liter engine delivered 85 brake horsepower at 2,250 rpm. Two wheelbases were offered: 144 and 150.5 inches. The suspension used semi-elliptic springs in front, cantilevered semi-elliptic springs in the rear. The last Springfield Silver Ghost carried serial number S403RL.

In 1926, Rolls-Royce introduced the New Phantom on two wheelbases, 143.5 and 146.5 inches. This car would later be renamed the Phantom I. Springfield undertook production of the New Phantom alongside the Silver Ghost, even though the two were priced within a couple of thousand dollars of each other. New Phantom production reached 12 per week in September 1929. One month later, the stock market crashed.

J. S. Inskip, who would become famous to postwar Americans as the importer of Rolls-Royce and most of the popular British sports cars, took over as president of Rolls-Royce of America in 1931. In the 10 years of the company's production until then, 2,944 American Rolls-Royces had been built, with 1,701 of them Silver Ghosts and 1,241 New Phantoms.

In 1929, a Phantom I with a Hibbard & Darrin convertible sedan body was priced at $19,665 at the Springfield factory.

Springfield was rocked by the response when Rolls-Royce introduced the Phantom II in Britain. The American plant simply couldn't afford to tool up for the new car. As many as 100 Phantom Is were built as late as 1932, when the PII was in full production and the PI was only a memory in Britain.

By 1934, Brewster began building custom bodies on Fords. When Rolls-Royce of England complained about this arrangement, Rolls-Royce of America changed the name of the company to the Springfield Manufacturing Company and contracted to import Rolls-Royces. The company went bankrupt in 1935.

While information on the date that the last Rolls-Royce was built in the United States hasn't been found, it is known that new cars were being sold as late as 1935.

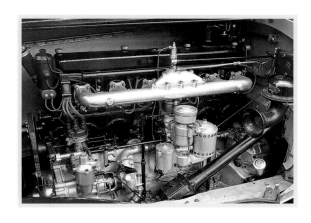

TOP LEFT • All Phantom IIs were built in England. The Chaplin car exhibits classic big convertible styling.

TOP MIDDLE • The trunk of the Chaplin Phantom II was square and held a significant amount of luggage.

TOP RIGHT • Chaplin's Phantom II convertible used a 120 hp 7.7-liter inline six-cylinder engine attached to a four-speed gearbox.

LEFT • Actor Charlie Chaplin once owned this 1931 Rolls-Royce Phantom II Brewster-bodied convertible. The center-mounted instruments made it easy to convert from right-hand-drive to left-hand-drive, although Rolls-Royce never converted their cars.

THE PHANTOMS

CLOCKWISE FROM TOP:
The interior of the 1933 Barker Phantom II Tourer had red upholstery. The body was polished aluminum.

This Phantom II engine is from a 1934 Fixed Head Coupe by Hooper. The Phantom II had a 7.7-liter inline six that developed an estimated 120 horsepower; 130 in the Continental.

This 1933 Phantom II four-seater Tourer by Barker was supplied to the Rajah Sahib of Hathawar. Note the twin Grebel scuttle spot lamps.

One of the most interesting bodies on a Rolls-Royce Phantom I was this boat-tail tourer built in 1924 by Labourdette of Paris

IN 1925 THE NEW PHANTOM WAS INTRODUCED TO THE ROLLS-ROYCE STABLE. WHEN LATER PHANTOMS WERE INTRODUCED THE CAR WAS RETROACTIVELY NAMED PHANTOM I, BUT, AS WITH THE JAGUAR MARK II, THERE NEVER REALLY WAS A MARK I, NOR WAS THERE EVER OFFICIALLY A PHANTOM I.

BELOW • The Labourdette boat-tail tourer moved the passengers (and the side mount) to the rear. Passengers in the back seat had their own windscreen as in a dual cowl phaeton.

RIGHT • At the opposite end of the styling spectrum from the boat-tail tourer was this Hooper-bodied 1926 Limousine de Ville on a Phantom I chassis.

BOTTOM RIGHT • At the rear of the Limousine de Ville was a luggage compartment that held three fitted suitcases.

PHANTOM I (THE NEW PHANTOM)

Technically, the New Phantom wasn't a new model at all, either. In fact Rolls-Royce even referred to it by the official designation of the Silver Ghost, 40/50. The factory even defended the use of the Silver Ghost engine in the New Phantom. "We were preparing a V-12 engine, a straight-eight, and an overhead camshaft six," the factory said. "Such engines have been built and tested. We have even looked into the techniques of supercharging." But, whatever the future promises said, still the factory felt that the inline six was the best choice for the Phantom. After almost 20 years of development, though, the six should have been refined to its utmost. And indeed it was. The highly critical British motoring press noted that the engine was essentially silent, emitting

only a whisper at 80 mph. (The media also complained about a latch on the gear lever that had to be released before the driver could shift gears.)

So the engine for the New Phantom was the Silver Ghost inline six, with a few modifications. While the block was still made up of two pairs of three cylinders, there was now a one-piece, cast-iron, detachable cylinder head covering the entire unit. It had a side-mounted camshaft that operated vertical overhead valves. The New Phantom engine also used dual ignition and a Rolls-Royce carburetor.

By 1928, the combustion chamber had a new shape and the spark plugs were relocated. No longer side by side, they were now located facing each other. The plugs

on the left side of the engine were fired by the magneto, on the right side by coil and battery power.

The compression ratio was raised from 4.0:1 to 4.2:1 in 1928, too, giving a slight increase in power. As with all Rolls-Royce engines, power output was not disclosed. However, the original power rating of the New Phantom was estimated to be 100 horsepower at 2,250 rpm. Power was relative, of course. It was possible to start a New Phantom off in third gear in total smoothness. On the road, the driver rarely had to shift out of fourth.

Engine temperature was controlled by a manual remote control of vertical radiator shutters. In the Silver Ghost, thermostatic control of coolant temperature was used. Rolls-Royce returned to thermostatic control in later years, but drivers of the New Phantom were advised to keep a watchful eye on the temperature readout on the dash.

Because the power output of the engine was considerable, larger and heavier custom bodies could be constructed without a significant loss of performance.

New Phantoms usually rode on high-pressure, narrow-section tires, despite the recent introduction of balloon tires. Balloon tires gave a softer ride, but the combination of low pressure and wide cross section made steering difficult. With narrow tread high-pressure tires, steering was much easier.

New Phantom buyers could choose between steel-spoked artillery wheels and Dunlop wire wheels. In the mid-1920s, aluminum wheel discs that were attached to the rims and painted to match the car would cover the wire wheels. These tended to make the car look more massive, but they also rattled.

Two wheelbase lengths were offered, 144 and 150.5 inches. There was a £50 premium for the longer wheelbase over the £1,800 chassis price.

Top speed was never the prime reason for owning a Rolls-Royce. Henry Royce himself is reported to have said, "High speed is for people who drive other cars. In one of our cars, one isn't risking one's head."

Still, a few special New Phantoms were constructed with higher speeds in mind. Barker built one lightweight body off a Robotham design that was used by Ivan Evernden, head of the Derby design office, on a trip to France to visit Royce at Le Canadel.

Three sports cars were built resembling a lightweight touring chassis car, 10EX, which turned a lap of 89 mph at Brooklands. Hooper and Jarvis built copies of this car and Barker built a third. While these weren't production cars per se, they were granted EX (for experimental) chassis numbers. Officially called Open Streamlined tourers, these cars were known inside the Derby works as Continentals, because only the better roads of the Continent would be a practical home for the performance they could achieve. And with Henry Royce ensconced on the Riviera, and less than two weeks between visits from someone at Derby, there was ample opportunity for these cars to stretch their legs.

With seating for four, the tourer also had a tonneau to cover the rear seat if there were no passengers back there. The windshield was a low V-shaped affair with a wiper on the driver's side only. The rear had a decided "boat-tail" look.

As we saw in the previous chapter, Springfield also built New Phantoms. While the Derby version was introduced in May 1925, it wasn't until August 1926 that the New Phantom became available in the United States. Part of the delay was caused by the exchange of drawings, memos, and reports to convert the right-hand-drive New Phantom into the left-hand-drive Springfield New Phantom. The gearbox and shift linkage had to be rebuilt, then thoroughly tested in accordance with standard Rolls-Royce practice.

Springfield New Phantoms did have central chassis lubrication, something that wasn't available on the Derby versions. Central lubrication supplied grease to 44 points on the chassis.

Exterior differences between the Springfield and Derby New Phantoms were in the headlights and bumpers. Springfield used large drum-shaped headlights similar to those used on the Silver Ghost, while Derby used more modern Lucas or Zeiss reflector lamps. Springfield-built cars also had bumpers, a feature Henry Royce never liked.

Rolls-Royce also suggested that spare tires be mounted in the rear for better weight distribution. However, American drivers preferred side-mounted spares. Therefore, very few cars left Springfield without this "non-factory-approved" feature.

The New Phantom hastened the demise of Springfield. The cost of retooling for the new model was disastrous. While other manufacturers could absorb retooling costs in high volume, Springfield built only 1,225 New Phantom cars in five years.

When the company folded, some of the employees found work in Detroit. The chief engineer, Maurice Olley, went to Cadillac, and joined the experimental department. He returned to England to work for Vauxhall. During World War II he was drafted by the Ministry of Supply, where he became a liaison engineer with Packard, which was building Rolls-Royce Merlin aircraft engines for American fighters.

GLITCH HITCH

Because of an error (today it would be called a computer glitch), the first 66 Springfield New Phantoms were built without front brakes, even though the British version of the car was so equipped. The wrong front axles were brought to the assembly line and these weren't compatible with the addition of front brakes. The rear-brake-only cars were later recalled to have front brakes fitted.

FAR LEFT TOP • With its top down, the split rear windshield of the 1928 Rolls-Royce Phantom I Grosvenor open tourer is obvious. Such windshields made rear-seat riding more comfortable.

FAR LEFT BOTTOM • When the Grosvenor car was restored, all the brightwork was re-nickel plated, including the large headlamps.

LEFT • The Grosvenor coachwork on this 1928 Phantom I chassis was the ultimate open tourer design and was probably the style most copied on replica cars.

PHANTOM II

The 1929 Phantom II was the last complete vehicle for
which Henry Royce was responsible. Members of the
design team included A. G. Elliott and Ken Jenner, who
were responsible for the engine; William Hardy and
Bernard Day, who were responsible for the chassis; and
Ivan Evernden, who was responsible for body engineering and coachwork design. Ernest Hives headed the test
department at Derby and received the first prototype,
18EX, in November 1928. Because of the secrecy involved,
a body by Barker was built separately, then fitted to the
car later. It had a chromed radiator shell, a new-fangled
idea brought over from the United States.

The first Phantom II test car began a 9,000-mile
endurance test in France on December 16, 1928. Even
after covering an average of 500 miles a day, no weak
points were discovered. By January 1929, any minor
defects had been corrected and the car was ready for
production. The car was officially introduced in
September 1929, on the cusp of the Great Depression.

One significant difference between the Phantom I
(PI) and Phantom II (PII) was in the low-slung frame of
PII. This improved roadholding significantly. The PII
also had hydraulic shock absorbers that could be
adjusted with a lever on the steering wheel. After 1933, a
hydraulic pump that was driven by the gearbox
provided automatic adjustment of the shock absorbers
as a function of speed.

Where the PI used a separate gearbox, torque-tube
drive, and cantilevered rear springs, the PII had an
integral engine and gearbox, Hotchkiss drive, hypoid
bevel rear axle, and semi-elliptic rear springs.

As with the PI, manually operated radiator
shutters controlled the coolant temperature.

ABOVE • This 1928 Phantom II prototype showed dual cowl phaeton styling on the new low-slung frame of the car.

LEFT • H.J. Mulliner built this Limousine body on a 1930 Rolls-Royce Phantom II chassis. The doors were hinged front and rear to provide easy entry and egress.

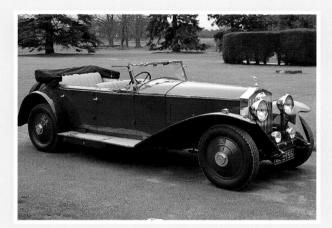

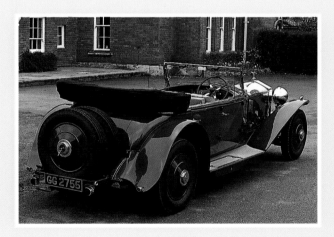

TOP • This 1930 Barker-bodied Phantom II Tourer had a more sweeping fender line than a similar Phantom I model. Note the disc wheels that were placed over the wire wheels for ease of cleaning.

BOTTOM • Like all Phantom IIs, this Barker-bodied 1930 Tourer was equipped with a series of silencers (mufflers) that reduced the exhaust note to a whisper.

ABOVE • **This 1930 Barker-bodied Rolls-Royce Phantom II Sedanca de Ville was a huge car with wheelbase lengths of 144 or 150 inches.**

RIGHT • **The Sedanca de Ville offered rear compartment passengers exceptional comfort and a measure of privacy.**

BOTTOM LEFT • **In the rear of the Phantom II Sedanca de Ville were two lockable storage compartments that were often used as liquor cabinets.**

BOTTOM RIGHT • **The only notification trailing drivers had of the Phantom II's stopping were license plate-mounted brake lights.**

The PII engine was essentially the same as in the PI, an inline six-cylinder built up of two three-cylinder blocks. The compression ratio was increased to 4.75:1 in 1929 and reached 5.0:1 in 1931. Power for the 7,668-cc engine was estimated at 120 to 130 horsepower. Other engine modifications to the PII included a reworked manifold which allowed for better breathing, and a modified head in which intake and exhaust valves were on opposite sides, matching the spark plugs.

Two wheelbase lengths were available, 144 and 150 inches, with a complete chassis length of 207 inches. That's before the body was placed on it. The short-wheelbase version had a chassis list price of £1,850, with the long-wheelbase version £50 more. Custom coachwork could cost another £800 to £1,000.

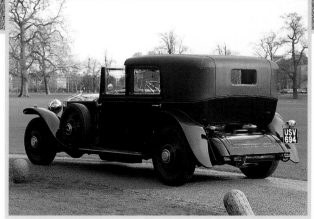

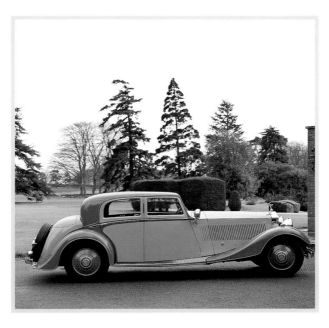

DOING THE CONTINENTAL

Rolls-Royce borrowed a name from the PI and created a Phantom II Continental for customers who preferred high-speed driving. Built on the short-wheelbase chassis, the Continental also had quicker steering and stiffer springs. Instead of the 20-inch wheels on the PII, the Continental rode on 19-inch wheels and, later, 17-inchers. The Continental also had a more powerful engine, thanks in part to larger inlet valves and higher compression. Fewer than 280 of the total 1,672 Phantom II examples were Continentals.

C. S. Shoup and T. E. Reich wrote about the Continental in *Rolls-Royce: Fact and Legend*:

"All passengers were brought within the wheelbase dimensions in construction of coachwork on these chassis: special springs were used, and the spare wheel or wheels were often mounted at the rear rather than in the front fender wells. These cars achieved an actual timed speed of 90 mph with full equipment and relatively heavy enclosed coachwork, all beyond 2½ tons in weight."

BELOW • **This 1937 Phantom II Sports Sedan by Barker showed the softer styling influences that were becoming obvious in the late 1930s.**

In October 1935, Rolls-Royce introduced the third Phantom to the public. Three and a half years were spent on developing prototypes and testing them, usually on French roads. The code name for these cars was Spectre, fitting for a Phantom. These cars were built only at Derby and all with right-hand drive.

The era of the 1930s was one of multiple cylinders. Cadillac, Packard, Duesenberg, and Mercedes-Benz all had cars with V engines of 12 or 16 cylinders. It was time for Rolls-Royce to enter the game. The engineers at Derby felt a V-12 was the best choice for their cars. Indeed, a V-12 has all the inherent balance properties of a straight-six, except there are two of them connected at the crankshaft.

Rolls-Royce had experience with V-12 engines because the company had been building aircraft engines of this configuration. A 60° V was chosen because it offered even firing intervals with a relatively simple crankshaft.

Despite the experience, an all-new design was chosen. Rolls-Royce used an aluminum block with steel wet liners. With a bore and stroke of 3.25 x 4.5 inches, the engine displaced 7.3 liters and developed an estimated 120 horsepower. Twin electric fuel pumps brought fuel from the gas tank to the engine.

TOP · **Compared with the Phantom II Limousine, this Phantom III Sedanca de Ville shows a modern invention for 1936—an enclosed trunk.**

MIDDLE · **Rear passengers in the Phantom III Sedanca de Ville had crystal bud vases and a fold-down arm rest for easy chair comfort.**

BOTTOM · **In contrast to the rear passengers, the chauffeur could drive with the hood up or down.**

ABOVE RIGHT · **Succeeding the Phantom II in 1935 was the Phantom III, with a 7.3-liter V-12 engine. This 1936 Sedanca de Ville was built on a 142-inch wheelbase chassis.**

The PIII chassis was also new for Rolls-Royce. Only one wheelbase—142 inches—was offered. The chassis used an X-frame that was welded, not riveted as in earlier cars. The rear suspension used semi-elliptic leaf springs, while the front used upper and lower triangular arms (double wishbones) with coil springs in an oil bath. All four wheels had hydraulic shock absorbers that were automatically controlled. There was a pedal for one-shot lubrication, while beneath the passenger's seat were the controls for the hydraulic jacks. Dunlop tires were mounted on 18-inch wheels.

Rolls-Royce suggested to its owners that they not exceed 75–80 mph. The engine was tested at Derby, however, at full throttle for hours with no problems, so, if an owner was rash enough to attempt the same thing, there should be no problem. But the factory didn't recommend it. Top speed, as tested by *The Autocar* in 1936, was 91.9 mph, with 0–60 mph taking 16.8 seconds.

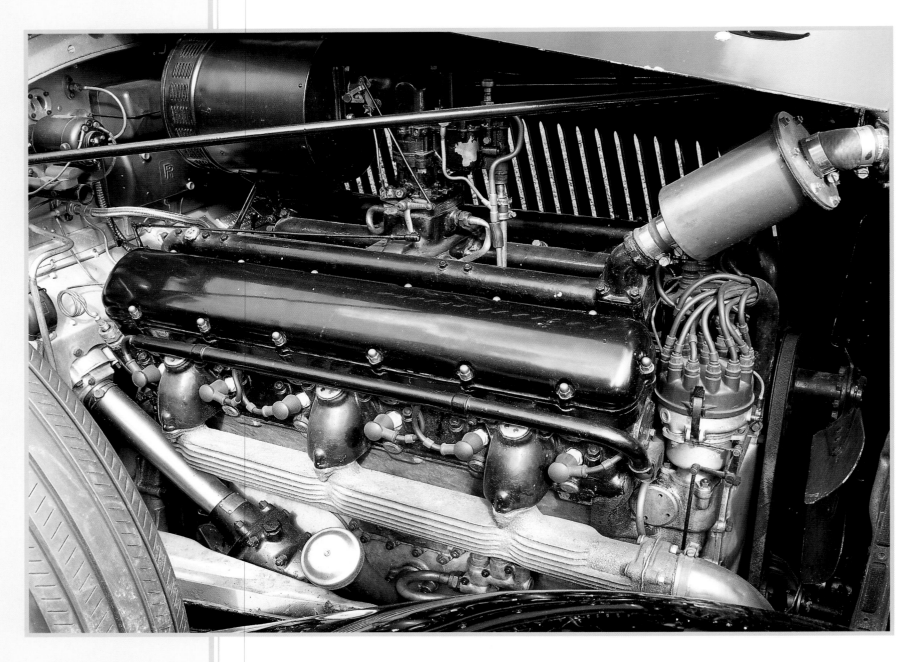

ABOVE • The 1937 Phantom II Barker-bodied Sports Sedan was powered by a 7.3-liter V-12 that developed an estimated 120 hp.

LEFT • The 1937 Phantom III Sports Sedan by Barker shows aerodynamic rear styling similar to that introduced by Cadillac on a V-16 Aero-Dynamic Coupe at the Chicago Exhibition in 1933.

Despite the fact that Daimler supplied the official state vehicles of the King, members of the royal family did order Phantom IIIs. Factory data shows that 130 cars were delivered to members of royal households and families of high-ranking nobility throughout the world.

Only 710 Phantom II models were produced between 1935 and 1939. Many of these vehicles were supplied with some of the finest coachwork on any Rolls-Royces.

This is the model that set the record for the fastest time from Algeria to Kano, Nigeria, by crossing the Sahara desert. The 2,200-mile run was completed in three days, 7½ hours.

By far the least popular Phantom, in terms of production, was the Phantom IV, built from 1950 to 1955. But it may have been the most popular in terms of prestige. Only 18 Phantom IV models were produced, with the majority going to royalty. The genesis of the PIV came in 1950, when an order was received from the royal family for a vehicle on an extra-long chassis. This vehicle was to be for Princess Elizabeth (soon to be Queen Elizabeth II) and the Duke of Edinburgh.

To create this special vehicle, the wheelbase of the then-current Silver Wraith was extended one foot from its maximum, of 133 inches to 145 inches. The limousine body that was placed on this chassis was itself extra-length, reaching an overall length of 230.3 inches. By comparison, the longest modern sedan is the Ford Crown Victoria and its brothers at 212 inches. This vehicle was also 76 inches wide and 78.8 inches tall. It was delivered to Buckingham Palace on June 6, 1950.

Powering the car was a 5.7-liter straight-eight that delivered an estimated 145 horsepower. The transmission was a four-speed manual with synchromesh on the top three gears. An automatic transmission was fitted to some later models. As well as all this, the car had a wheel diameter of 17 inches. This extraordinary vehicle was ultimately named Phantom IV.

Hooper built six bodies for Phantom IVs, H. J. Mulliner 10. Franay of Paris built a body on a PIV chassis for Prince Talal al Saud Ryal of Saudi Arabia. The final body was built by Rolls-Royce, but it stayed in company hands. These bodies had power windows and some had automatic transmissions.

The last Phantom IV, an all-black Hooper-bodied limousine, was delivered to the Shah of Iran on December 29, 1955.

ABOVE LEFT • **This 1937 Phantom III Sedanca exhibits "bustle back" styling that was duplicated 43 years later in the Cadillac Seville. The Phantom III also rode on wide section 18-inch diameter tires.**

ABOVE • **All Phantom IV chassis were designated for standing royalty and only 18 were produced. This 1950 Phantom IV was identical to one delivered to Buckingham Palace in June 1950.**

PHANTOMS V AND VI

A new Phantom was introduced in 1959 that was to be for business and political leaders, but not reserved for heads of state. The Phantom V remained in production for nine years, during which time 832 were produced.

Power for the PV came from a 6.2-liter 90° aluminum V-8 that sent between 200 and 215 horsepower. It delivered its power to the rear wheels through a four-speed GM/Rolls-Royce automatic transmission. Chassis for the PV were built on a 144-inch wheelbase and reached 238 inches in length and a width of 79 inches.

Rolls-Royce used power-assisted drum brakes on all four wheels. The suspension was independent in front with semi-elliptic leaf springs in the rear. As had been standard for many years, the Phantom V featured automatic shock-absorber control.

Bodies were built by Park Ward, James Young, Mulliner Park Ward, Hooper, and Chapron. The first cars to appear were limousines from Mulliner Park Ward. Most had interior partitions between the driver and passenger compartment. Body styling differed primarily in the treatment of the rear of the car. Some customers didn't want the extra side window, some wanted a higher-mounted trunk lid, and some wanted a smaller rear window. Halwart Schrader in *Rolls-*

Royce Cars and Bentley from 1931 notes, "The James Young bodies had more prominent rear bumper lines. The amount of armor plate and bulletproof glass that went into the bodies built for Marshal Tito, General Trujillo, King Hassan II of Morocco or President Bourguiba of Tunisia, was cloaked in professional discretion." One James Young car shows a definite "bustle back" design.

Park Ward built a "Canberra" limousine for Queen Elizabeth II that was almost six feet tall, approximately five inches taller than the "standard" PV. This car also had a Plexiglas section fitted into the roof and another in the rear panel. The bumpers could be removed if the car had to be airlifted or shipped by sea to a location the Queen might be visiting.

The Italian coachbuilder Frua built one convertible on a Phantom V chassis.

The royal court again ordered Phantom Vs, as Rolls-Royce finally displaced Daimler as the official vehicle.

Two of these were reserved for the Queen and her family, while the remainder belonged to the government, ambassadors and the Buckingham Palace fleet.

Phantom Vs continued to be produced until 1968.

The final Phantom (until now) was the Phantom VI, introduced in 1968. The PVI was in production for more than 20 years. The only exterior difference between the intake at the base of the windshield on the higher-numbered car. In some circles, the Phantom VI is known as a "modified Phantom V."

The PVI was slightly smaller than the PV, though. Built on a 140.9-inch wheelbase, the Phantom VI was still 238 inches long overall. Equipped with power steering, the long car could be steered with the fingertips. However, tight turns were its bane, because it had a turning-circle diameter of 53.5 feet, making it less than nimble on its 8.90-by-15-inch tires.

Ride comfort, as intended, was excellent. As did its predecessor, the Phantom VI had a rigid rear axle located by semi-elliptic leaf springs. The front suspension was independent and the shock absorbers

BY ROYAL APPOINTMENT

After Princess Elizabeth and the Duke of Edinburgh put the Phantom IV into service, orders came gushing in from other heads of state and royalty of other nations for similar vehicles. The Shah of Iran ordered one, as did the Sheikh of Kuwait, the Aga Khan, King Faisal II of Egypt, and Prince Abdullah of Iraq. General Franco of Spain ordered three with bulletproof glass. Three more were built for England's royal court and three more for Kuwait.

Queen Elizabeth II used a Hooper-bodied Phantom IV landaulette for her coronation in 1953. The car was painted claret and black for the occasion. While this vehicle was owned by Rolls-Royce, it became property of the Crown in 1959. The landau top proved to be difficult because it could not be raised or lowered while the car was in motion.

could be adjusted hydraulically. Drum brakes were located at all four wheels.

Two engines were offered. For the first 10 years of its existence, the Phantom VI was equipped with a 6.3-liter V-8 that delivered an estimated 200 horsepower. The transmission was a four-speed automatic transmission of GM/Rolls-Royce Turbo Hydra-Matic design. From 1978 onward, the engine was a 6.8-liter V-8 rated at an estimated 200 horsepower. The gearbox was three-speed GM/Rolls-Royce automatic. The Phantom VI weighted 6,050 pounds, even with aluminum body panels. Still, the larger engine, according to a road test by the Swiss magazine *Automobil Revue*, could propel the PVI from 0–60 mph in 14.5 seconds.

Rear seats were made of the highest-quality leather with copious amounts of wood trim. Two jump seats folded out of the way at the feet of the rear passengers. The chauffeur (Phantoms were rarely owner-driven) sat on a bench seat that didn't offer a lot of leg or chest room. But ultimately the chauffeur's job was to drive the car, not to enjoy the ride.

There were few special-bodied Phantom VIs. One two-door Frua cabriolet was built for a diplomat living in Geneva. Some works-bodied limousines were delivered to Africa. And a special raised-roof body was built for Queen Elizabeth in 1977 on the 25th anniversary of her coronation.

TOP • **The Phantom VI, slightly smaller than the Phantom V and riding on 15-inch tires, was still a substantial automobile.**

MIDDLE • **With its taller passenger compartment, the Phantom VI State Limousine was somewhat ungainly.**

BOTTOM • **This Phantom VI State Limousine was commissioned by the British motor industry as a Jubilee gift for Queen Elizabeth II in 1977.**

CLOCKWISE FROM TOP:
Walter Owen (W.O.) Bentley felt he had a calling in the locomotive. He built his first car in 1917.

Bentley's winged 'B' badge rivals any other manufacturer's in longevity and honor.

Bentley's winged mascot had a greater sporting reputation than the Rolls-Royce Spirit of Ecstasy. It was retained in modified form after Rolls-Royce bought Bentley.

The 1929 Bentley 4-½ Liter 'Blower Bentley' was powerful, but its lack of reliability kept it from winning races.

IN MANY WAYS, BENTLEY WAS MUCH LIKE ROLLS-ROYCE. BOTH MARQUES FEATURED CARS THAT WERE DESIGNED BY PERFECTIONISTS, MEN WHO DEMANDED ONLY THE BEST. LIKE HENRY ROYCE, WALTER OWEN BENTLEY (KNOWN ALWAYS AS W. O.) WOULD HAVE HIS NAME LIVE ON IN THE PROGENY OF THE PRODUCTS HE DESIGNED. W. O. SAID HE FELT HE HAD A "CALLING, A VOCATION," AND NO ONE WAS GOING TO STOP HIM. THIS CALLING WAS THE LOCOMOTIVE. HE BECAME AN APPRENTICE FOR THE GREAT NORTHERN RAILWAY AT THE AGE OF 16. AFTER THAT HE BECAME FASCINATED WITH MOTORCYCLES. AFTER FIVE YEARS WITH THE RAILROAD, HE DEVELOPED A PASSION FOR THE INTERNAL-COMBUSTION ENGINE AND CHANGED HIS LIFE'S DEDICATION TO CAR ENGINES.

In 1912, W. O. and his brother Henry ran an import agency for three French cars. Among these was one known as the DFP. This was a sports car, but it wasn't a very good sports car. The initials stood for Doriot, Flandrin, et Parant, but it was known as *dernière fer-raille parisienne* ("the latest scrap iron from Paris"). W. O., however, raced a DFP and finished sixth in the 1914 Tourist Trophy.

From 1915 to 1917, Bentley worked for a company that built aircraft engines. He persuaded the company to copy a Mercedes racing engine to use in naval airplanes. Their breakthrough product was a radial engine with aluminum pistons, the BR1.

During World War I, Bentley became a squadron leader in the Royal Flying Corps. After the Armistice, he returned to civilian life and began designing and building sports cars. His first effort was a three-liter, four-cylinder-engined model that had a single overhead camshaft and four valves per cylinder. After two years of modifications and alterations, Bentley felt the car was ready for production.

He showed the car at the 1919 London Motor Show. The first test reports were published in 1920. But it wasn't until 1921 that people were able to purchase a Bentley automobile. The Bentley 3-Litre was available in Standard or Speed versions. Unlike a Rolls-Royce, however, here was an automobile whose deep, rich sound announced its power. As Halwart Schrader writes in *Rolls-Royce Cars and Bentley from 1931*, "the engine noise played a vital role in the make-up of the Bentley's character."

In competition, Bentley found its most formidable rival in the French Bugatti. Bentleys achieved notable success on the race circuits of Europe, just like Bugatti. And, like Bugatti, the cars of W. O. Bentley were, according to Schrader, "clean and functional in concept and design, with superior performance, and perfect finish."

According to the record books, Frank Clement was the first Bentley driver to achieve a victory, in the Junior Sprint Handicap at Brooklands in Surrey in May 1921.

At the first LeMans race, the winners were André Lagache and René Leonard in a Chenard-Walcker. The only Bentley, a 3-Litre, was handicapped by racing in the rain without front brakes, but still finished fourth. John Duff and Frank Clement were the first to earn honors at LeMans with that fourth-place finish in 1923.

Duff had owned a Bentley dealership in London. He prepared his own 3-Litre and set several new speed records at Brooklands. When he called the company to ask for assistance in running the LeMans race,

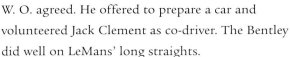

W. O. agreed. He offered to prepare a car and volunteered Jack Clement as co-driver. The Bentley did well on LeMans' long straights.

Duff and Clement won the race in 1924 (with four-wheel brakes), covering 1,260 miles. Of the 40 starters, only 17 finished. This win encouraged W. O. to enter a team in the famous 24-hour race. Bentleys, driven by the famed "Bentley Boys," won the 24 hours of LeMans from 1927 to 1930. The series of wins began with the 3-Litre.

In the 1926 race, the editor of *The Autocar*, S. C. H. "Sammy" Davis, was asked to co-drive by J. D. "Benjy" Benjafield, a medical specialist who knew little about cars but was a fast driver. The two had problems with

rain and failing brakes in 1926 but they returned as a team in 1927. Driving a 3-Litre known as "Old No. 7," they won. During the race there was a multicar accident, which eliminated all the other Bentleys on the team. Benjafield and Davis saw their car damaged as well, but they continued on in the rain. They slowly worked their way up the field until through dogged perseverance they won the race.

In 1927, Bentley replaced the 3-Litre with the 4.5-Litre. This car won the 1928 race at LeMans with Captain Woolf Barnato driving. Next was the 6.5-Litre, known as the Speed Six. In LeMans racing trim this car generated 150 horsepower as well as robust strength. It won in 1929 and 1930. In 1929, Barnato

TOP LEFT • **1926 Bentley 3 Litre Speed model with body by Barker, was the basis for the racer to its right.**

TOP • **This 1926 Bentley Le Mans team car was the only nine-foot wheelbase car to compete in the race. The following year, Bentley began its four-year winning streak.**

BOTTOM • **W.O. Bentley's 3-liter engine was a four-cylinder configuration with a single overhead camshaft and four valves per cylinder.**

and Sir Henry "Tim" Birkin drove a Speed Six and led from the start. Their only competition was from three other 4.5-Litre Bentleys, but they were all more than 70 miles behind them. It was Barnato's third straight win.

Barnato drove with Glen Kidston in 1930. Kidston was a former navy officer. He was a survivor, having been the only person to emerge alive from the crash of a London–Paris airliner and later freeing his submarine from the mud at the bottom of the sea. In racing, he survived a crash in the 1929 Tourist Trophy motorcycle race. Kidston's luck ran out in 1931 when his de Havilland Moth biplane broke up in midair and crashed in Africa.

Tim Birkin developed a supercharged version of the 4.5-Litre. This car raced at LeMans but never

won, despite its 240 horsepower. Birkin did set a new lap record, however, for the Brooklands Outer Circuit where he achieved 138 mph.

Birkin was an ex-Royal Flying Corps pilot who would drive in flying goggles, white drill helmet, and silk scarf. His "Birkin Blowers" improved the performance of the Bentleys, but they were less reliable than the unsupercharged cars. Eventually, Birkin set up his own company to produce superchargers for Bentleys. He died of blood poisoning after burning his arm on an exhaust pipe at the 1933 Tripoli Grand Prix.

In the late 1920s. Bentley took on Harry Westlake as a consultant to help improve engine performance. Westlake was working for Automotive Products at the time and later did work on engines for Austin and Henry Lyons at SS Cars (later to become Jaguar).

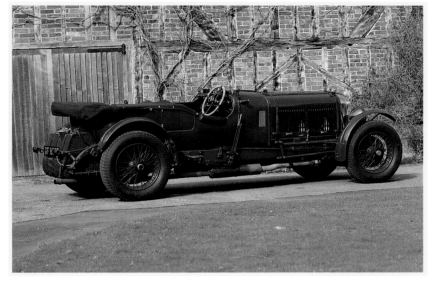

FAR LEFT TOP • One of the most famous Bentleys was the 'Blower Bentley,' a supercharged 4-½ liter 1928 model which developed 240 hp.

FAR LEFT BOTTOM • The supercharger developed by Tim Birkin increased horsepower but decreased reliability. With Birkin driving, a Blower Bentley set a new lap record at Brooklands at 138 mph.

LEFT TOP • Even though the supercharged 4-½ liter was an out-and-out racer, it still had all the trappings of a road car.

LEFT • 'Blower Bentleys' used a 4-½ liter inline six-cylinder engine similar to the one that powered the 1928 Le Mans winners.

ABOVE • This 1930 Bentley Speed Six won the 500-mile Brooklands in 1930 and finished second at Le Mans a month later. Speed Sixes were the ultimate Bentley racers.

SIBLING RIVALRY

Jack and Clive Dunfee were brothers who had to work hard to buy their cars. Both raced for other teams before being invited to join "The Bentley Boys." Jack finished second at LeMans in 1929 and won the 500-mile race at Brooklands in 1931. In the 1932 race, Jack and Clive shared a specially prepared eight-liter car that was the fastest in the race. Unfortunately, Clive flew over the top of the banking and was killed while he was driving. Jack never raced again.

STRIVING FOR IMPROVEMENT

Woolf Barnato was the chairman of Bentley from 1926 onward. Barnato was the son of Barney Barnato, who was born poor but rose to control the diamond mines in Kimberley, South Africa, with Cecil Rhodes. Barnato extended financial support to back Bentley when it ran into difficulties. He took over as chairman in 1929, but when the bleeding became terminal by 1931 he withdrew his investment.

Bentley's financial problems were caused by high manufacturing costs, low production numbers, and the upkeep of an active racing team. In all the years under W. O., fewer than 3,000 cars were produced. The 8-Litre supercar didn't help, and only 100 were built.

Bentley approached Napier, which was interested in buying his company. Napier's bid was accepted, but two days before the official sale date another offer came in for the company that was slightly higher than Napier's. When Napier tried to raise its offer, the bankruptcy court declined, saying it wasn't an auctioneer. The winning bid was by the British Equitable Trust, a cover for Rolls-Royce, who had beaten Napier to the punch and bought Bentley Motors and control of W. O. When Henry Royce commented to Bentley that he was surprised Bentley wasn't a trained engineer, Bentley countered by noting that he was trained as an engineer in a railway works, just as Royce had been.

The sad news for W. O. Bentley at Rolls-Royce was that he was not permitted to design cars and was used primarily in testing new models. He left Rolls-Royce and moved to Lagonda, where he regained his designing role and designed the Lagonda Rapide V12 model, which was intended as a challenger to the Rolls-Royce Phantom III. Bentley died in 1971.

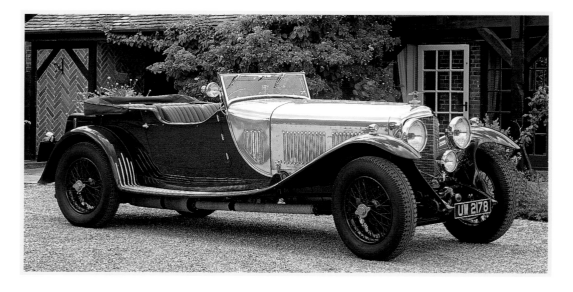

LEFT • While Bentley was winning races, it was also working to develop passenger cars. This 1929 Standard Six wears boat-tail coachwork by Barker.

BOTTOM LEFT • G. Wylder built this short-chassis Tourer on a 1930 Bentley Speed Six chassis. Note the similarity to the Barker-bodied cars.

BOTTOM • Removing the wheel of the 1929 Standard Six meant hammering the knock-off hub in the 'undo' direction.

BOTTOM RIGHT • Many consider the Speed Six to be the best of the 'old school' Bentleys. The six-cylinder engine developed 180 horsepower, only two less than the supercharged four.

THE BLUE TRAIN EXPRESS

Legendary racing cars are nothing without their legends. One of the more interesting involving Bentley is of the Blue Train Express, driven by Barnato, who would eventually take over the company.

Captain Barnato was at a cocktail party in Cannes, France, when the discussions turned to the subject of cars and racing. When the conversation drifted toward an advertisement by a manufacturer that their car could go faster than the Blue Train Express as it went from Cannes to Calais, Barnato said he could go one better on that claim. Driving his own Bentley Speed Six, he could arrive in

England before the Blue Train reached Calais. Braggadocio turned to challenge and the next evening at 5:54 pm the Blue Train and Barnato both left the station at Cannes, bound for Calais.

Barnato faced heavy rain at Lyons, missed a refueling stop in Auxerre, and had a flat near Paris, when they had to mount their only spare. They reached the coast at 10:30 am and crossed the Channel on a packet boat. They were parked outside the Conservative Club on St James's Street in London at 3:20 pm, four minutes before the Blue Train reached Calais. Barnato won his bet.

Sir Henry Royce had been developing a smaller car at his Le Canadel drafting room. This was to be a small, 2,364-cc, six-cylinder car, code name Peregrine. But this was a very un-Rolls-Royce type of car. Rolls-Royces were, as Don Vorderman said in *Automobile Quarterly*, "large, smooth, quiet, slow revving, understressed engines propelling big, roomy cars."

Peregrine was definitely underpowered, so it was decided to add a supercharger to boost output. After a 10,000-mile test on the Continent, it was discovered that the Peregrine engine would go through bearings at 5,000 rpm, yet it was the type of engine that needed sustained high revs for adequate performance. And performance never was adequate, since the engine developed only something like 75 horsepower.

The someone suggested putting the current 20/25 Rolls-Royce engine in the Peregrine chassis. They could call it a Bentley. As it turned out the car they concocted had exceptional performance, better than a Rolls-Royce.

Hence, the first Bentley to emerge after the union of Rolls-Royce and Bentley was the 1933 3.5-Litre, with an engine capacity of 3,669 cc, which was a counterpart to the Rolls-Royce 20/25. The engines of the two cars were the same, but the chassis were different. This car was called "The Silent Sports Car," and was aimed at owner-drivers who weren't necessarily the Rolls-Royce "type" but who still wanted a high-quality car.

Using the same Rolls-Royce 3.5-liter straight-six, the Bentley used two carburetors, while the Rolls used one. Top speed for "The Silent Sports Car" was a mere 85 mph, depending on the body style chosen. Bentley, like Rolls-Royce, sold only the chassis and let the buyer have a body built by the coachbuilder of choice. Most of the bodies built on the 126-inch wheelbase chassis were tourers and drop-head coupes. A few cars were built with closed bodywork, but limousines were impractical on such a short chassis.

The Bentley shared some of the features of the Rolls-Royce, such as centralized chassis lubrication and "Ride Control" shock-absorber adjustment on the steering wheel. Rolls-Royce built 1,191 3.5-Litre Bentleys at Crewe in northwest England.

Eddie Hall took delivery of one of the first 3.5-Litre chassis and had it fitted with racing bodywork. He used this car for reconnaissance runs of the Mille Miglia, but liked it so much he entered it in the 1934 Tourist Trophy race in Ireland. Hall finished second on handicap, but outran the field of Aston Martins, Lagondas, Frazer Nashes, and Rileys. Hall repeated his success in 1935 and again in 1936, when he completed the race in a 4¼-liter model.

In 1936, Rolls-Royce introduced the 25/30 model, and with it a new Bentley, labeled Four and a Quarter, or the 4.25-Litre. As with the 3.5-Litre, the main difference between the engines was in the carburetors. The Rolls-Royce used a single Stromberg, the Bentley twin SUs. Output for the Bentley was estimated at 120 horsepower; for the Rolls-Royce it was 105.

The 4.25-Litre's chassis was identical to the 3.5-Litre's and remained that way until the model was discontinued in 1939. Rolls-Royce produced 1,241 Bentley 4.25-Litre chassis. Owners would have bodies built by Vanden Plas, Gurney Nutting, Carlton, Windover, and Van Vooren.

A new Bentley, the M Series, went into production in October 1938. This car had a new gearbox, which included a direct-drive third gear and an overdrive fourth gear. With smaller-diameter and wider tires, the steering linkage was also modified and road handling improved. But M Series sales did not pick up because there were rumors of a new Bentley model on the horizon. This was to be the Mark V, which was introduced in the spring of 1939.

While production never got off the ground owing to the onset of World War II, production of the Mark V was scheduled to begin in October 1939. Fewer than 15 were built before production was halted by the war and, of these, maybe 10 were delivered to customers.

One 4.5-Litre prototype had a streamlined body fitted to it by Marcel Pourtot in France. This Georges Paulin design was for the Greek racer Nikky Embiricos. Paulin designed another streamlined coupé that was to be built by Van Vooren. These coupés received a new name, Corniche, to honor the new look. Van Vooren produced five copies, three of which were unfinished when war broke out.

Three other Mark V prototypes had straight-eight engines but never reached production.

LEFT • The 1953 R-Type Continental with body by Mulliner extended the art of aerodynamics beyond what most manufacturers of the era were offering. The sloping tail and enveloping body hid a 4.9-liter engine.

TOP • The Empress-style sedan shows Hooper's typical side coloring and an aerodynamic rear.

MIDDLE • Built on a Mk VI chassis, this 1952 Empress-style sedan by Hooper offered luxury approaching that of Rolls-Royce but little of the sportiness of earlier Bentleys.

BOTTOM • While Bentleys were better suited to be large sedans, Park Ward built this coupe body on a 1951 Mk VI chassis.

RIGHT • In contrast to the R-Type Continental, Bentley also offered a conventional R-Type Standard Steel Saloon with a less powerful engine.

THE POSTWAR BENTLEYS

After the war ended, Bentley was among the first to begin production. There was a new body shop erected next to the Crewe works and it was for Bentley, not Rolls-Royce. Rolls didn't use the facility until production of the Silver Dawn began in 1949. The body works produced a sedan body on the old Mark V chassis, now rechristened Mark VI. The Standard Steel Saloon proved popular, and 5,201 were produced before production halted in 1952 to make way for the R-Type.

Except for a shorter wheelbase (120 versus 124 inches) the prewar Mark V and the postwar Mark VI were identical with the Rolls-Royce Wraith. All had a box-section steel frame with cross bracing, independent front suspension, remote-controlled shock absorbers, power brakes, and a 4.3-liter, inline, six-cylinder engine.

Acceleration and top speed of the Mark VI were slightly better than those of the contemporary Silver Dawn because of a 420-pound weight advantage. The Bentley also had better fuel-consumption figures.

Introduced at the October 1952 London Motor Show at Earl's Court was the Bentley R-Type. This model became available in two versions: the Standard Steel Saloon and the Continental. While the Saloon had a conventional sedan body, the Continental coupe's body showed the influence of the prewar Paulin design in the Mark V. Pininfarina built two Continental bodies and Park Ward five, including one notchback design.

The Continental had a larger engine of 4.9 liters' capacity. Added power also came from a higher compression ratio (7.27:1 versus 6.4:1), larger SU carburetors, and a bigger radiator. For performance, the Continental had a close-ratio manual gearbox versus the automatic of the Saloon and a lower rear-axle ratio. The difference amounted to 15 horsepower, with the Continental reaching 165 horsepower. Both cars were built on the same 120-inch wheelbase. Rolls produced 2,320 R-Types and 208 R-Type Continentals before it was discontinued in 1955.

Next in line was the S1 of 1955–59, which was identical to the Rolls-Royce Silver Cloud. The bodies of both cars were lower and more aerodynamic, but the vehicles were essentially identical. Many observers felt that the body looked better with the smaller, rounder Bentley grille than it did with the Grecian columns of the larger Rolls-Royce grille.

In any case, the wheelbase stretched to 123 inches and overall length grew to 212 inches. Width was 74.5 inches and height 64 inches. In 1958 a long-wheelbase version of both the S1 and Silver Cloud was introduced at 127 inches. This was for people who wanted a chauffeur-driven car with a partition. S1 Continentals were also produced with aerodynamic custom bodies. A total of 431 S1 Continentals were built, compared with 3,027 with the short wheelbase and 35 with the long wheelbase.

Bentley's S2 ran from 1959 to 1962, during which time 1,865 short-wheelbase versions, 57 long-wheelbase versions, and 388 Continentals were built. The S2 and its companion, Silver Cloud II, shared a 6.2-liter V-8 engine. This engine was a pure Rolls-Royce creation, not a derivation of a General Motors V-8 design as it was considered to be. In that time, the bore/stroke ratio was changed, timing gears instead of a chain were substituted, and a Rolls-Royce ignition-lubrication system was used. A General Motors Dual-Range Hydra-Matic automatic transmission was standard, however.

H. J. Mulliner supplied fastback S2 Continental bodies. Only a bench front seat was available, but the seat backs were individually adjustable. Standard equipment also included small picnic tables built into the backs of the front seats for passenger comfort. There was also a line of Cabriolets bodies built that included power tops in their design.

The S3 came out in 1962 in conjunction with the Silver Cloud III. Engine changes included a new silicon-alloy cylinder head with a 9.0:1 compression ratio, larger carburetors, and modified valve timing. Power was increased to an estimated 275 horsepower. A Continental and a cabriolet built by James Young remained in the S3 program. In addition, a four-door Continental built by Mulliner was called the Flying Spur and had a rounded rear fender, very much in Jaguar style. All cars were distinguished by quad headlights.

FAR LEFT • **This view of the Mulliner 1953 R-Type Continental shows the fastback sweep of the roofline and a hint of tailfins.**

BOTTOM LEFT • **The S1 Continental replaced the R-Type in 1955. It was essentially identical to the Rolls-Royce Silver Cloud, as in this Mulliner-bodied example, but with the rounder Bentley grille.**

BOTTOM RIGHT • **The winged 'B' hood ornament and winged Bentley badge remained virtually unchanged from 1926 to this 1957 S1 Continental.**

LEFT • **Bentley introduced the S3 Continental in 1962. This drophead coupe is an especially fine example.**

ABOVE • **The 1958 S1 Continental Drophead Coupe with body by Park Ward was powered by an engine attached to a GM-designed automatic transmission.**

CLOCKWISE FROM TOP:
This 1955 Empress-style Silver Dawn with body by Hooper shows little evolution from the Silver Wraith, even down to the classic Hooper two-tone paint scheme.

All Rolls-Royces and Bentleys were built in this factory at Crewe from 1946 onwards.

Hooper bodied this 1946 Silver Wraith Limousine. The car was a direct descendent of the prewar Wraith, with essentially the same engine.

ROLLS-ROYCE CLOSED OUT THE PREWAR ERA WITH THE WRAITH, WHICH WAS THE NATURAL EXTENSION OF THE TWENTY INTRODUCED IN 1922. QUITE NATURALLY, THEN, ROLLS-ROYCE OPENED THE POSTWAR ERA WITH THE SILVER WRAITH, INTRODUCED IN 1946. EVEN THOUGH THE WAR HAD INTERVENED AND PRODUCTION HAD CEASED FOR SEVEN YEARS, ROLLS-ROYCE WAS NOT THE TYPE OF COMPANY TO MAKE RASH CHANGES.

FOR ONE, THE SILVER WRAITH'S ENGINE WAS ESSENTIALLY IDENTICAL TO THAT OF THE WRAITH. DISPLACEMENT WAS STILL 4,257 CC, WITH THE BORE AND STROKE UNCHANGED FROM THE PREWAR CAR.

Showing that classic body styles can span the years, Mulliner built this Sedanca de Ville on a 1947 Silver Wraith chassis.

The engine had been improved, though. One change was the shift to an F-head design, with overhead inlet valves and side exhaust valves. A camshaft located in the side of the block operated both. The cylinder bores were chrome-plated. Belts now drove both the water pump and the generator. The older system of five gears had been replaced as being too cumbersome and noisier than belts. Gears still drove the camshaft, however. Output was estimated at 120 horsepower.

In 1951, the six-cylinder engine was bored out again and the compression ratio increased from 6.4:1 to 6.75:1. The 4,566-cc engine that resulted from these changes now produced an estimated 135 horsepower, a bit less than the output of the Bentley that used the same engine. The engine was bored out once more in 1955, yielding 4,887 cc and approximately 160 horsepower.

These engines were connected to a four-speed manual transmission. However, primarily because of the influence of the American market, a General Motors automatic transmission was offered as an option after 1952. The automatic became standard in 1958.

Under the body was a chassis that was essentially unchanged from that of the Wraith. There were more welded joints than riveted and bolted joints, but other changes were minor. The independent front suspension was the same as in the Wraith. The biggest change was in the use of bolt-on pressed-steel wheels in place of wire wheels.

The first Silver Wraith chassis had a 127-inch wheelbase. A 133-inch wheelbase chassis was offered for limousine bodies with partitions. The long-wheelbase chassis used 7.50-by-16 tires instead of the 6.50-by-17 tires on the short-wheelbase version.

Custom bodies were still the order of the day with the Silver Wraith, but this was not the case for the cars that followed. The Silver Wraith was the last Rolls-Royce to be offered as a chassis only. Thus, bodies by Hooper, Mulliner, Park Ward, and Gurney Nutting were seen regularly on Silver Wraith chassis.

Rolls-Royce built 1,144 short-wheelbase Silver Wraiths and 639 with the long wheelbase. Thirty-six became hearses and one became a station wagon ("estate car"), delivered to an American customer.

THE SILVER DAWN

At the same time the Silver Wraith was the Silver Dawn, produced from 1949 to 1955. Primarily an export model, the Silver Dawn was introduced in October 1949 at the London Motor Show. The Silver Dawn rode on a shorter wheelbase than the Silver Wraith, 120 inches compared with 127 and 133 inches. It also came with a standard body, "the standard steel saloon", which was exactly the same as the Bentley, except for the grille. Park Ward built the bodies for the cars in London. Only 785 were produced.

Park Ward was building bodies for Silver Wraiths at the same time as for Silver Dawns. On the Wraiths, the plaque read "Coachwork by Park Ward." On the Dawn, "Coachwork by Rolls-Royce." Park Ward was, of course, now part of Rolls-Royce, but the exclusivity of the name was still reserved for more expensive models.

TOP LEFT · Under the hood of the Silver Dawn was the old inline six, bored out to 4.9 liters and producing about 160 hp.

LEFT · The Silver Dawn interior reflected traditional Rolls-Royce elegance, with center-mounted instruments to ease the transition from right-hand drive to left-hand drive.

BOTTOM LEFT · The Rolls-Royce grille showed little change over the years, although the Spirit hood ornament was now kneeling and the headlights were receding into the body.

BOTTOM RIGHT · Rolls-Royce produced the Silver Dawn from 1949 to 1955. In the last year, Hooper built this Empress-style body on a Dawn chassis.

The Silver Dawn was the first Rolls-Royce to come out of new manufacturing facilities at Crewe. The engine was the same as in the Silver Wraith, a 4,257-cc, 120-horsepower six up to 1951, and the bored-out 4,566-cc, 135-horsepower six from 1951 to 1955. The transmission was the General Motors-designed Hydra-Matic with the shifter on the steering column.

The Autocar tested a Silver Dawn with a "big-bore" engine in 1953, it achieved a top speed of 86.5 mph and fuel consumption of 12 to 14 miles per gallon.

The Autocar tested the Silver Dawn and generally praised the car. However, the magazine had some comments about the single-body design. "When only one body type is offered, many wishes must be met, and such a design must therefore be something of a compromise, and the Silver Dawn body is a compromise."

Coachbuilders did rebody Silver Dawns. H. J. Mulliner created a two-door cabriolet and James Young built a limousine.

Rolls-Royce used the X-frame that had been developed for the prewar Wraith and changed slightly for the Silver Wraith. Welding of the frame members was found to be unsatisfactory, however, and the cross members were now riveted to the side members. New welding techniques meant welded frames returned in 1953, which gave the frames added rigidity.

While it didn't have built-in jacks, the Silver Dawn did have centralized chassis lubrication. It was the first Rolls-Royce with two-speed windshield wipers, and also had folding picnic tables in the back of the front seats, and another small tray below the instrument panel, like previous cars. It also had single-key locking, a steel sunroof, and electrically heated rear windows.

VIP CUSTOMERS

The first Silver Wraith became the official car of the Mayor of Derby. It wore a body by H. J. Mulliner and was delivered in August 1947. Princess Elizabeth is credited with being the first to receive a Silver Wraith, however. Hers was chassis number 14 (no Rolls-Royce chassis ever had a 13 as the final two digits in its chassis number). With a body by Hooper, Princess Elizabeth's Silver Wraith was delivered for Christmas 1946.

Chassis 5 with a Hooper limousine body was on display at the 1947 Geneva Motor Show. Among the customers who placed orders at the show for Silver Wraiths were the Sultan of Morocco, the movie executive Sir Alexander Korda, and the Magistrate of Johannesburg. The oil billionaire Nubar Gulbenkian ordered a Silver Wraith with a Mulliner Sedanca de Ville body. Gulbenkian also bought a four-door cabriolet in 1953.

The last Silver Wraith delivered was a Hooper-bodied long-wheelbase sedan, which went to the embassy of the Republic of Ghana in Germany in 1959. Production officially ended in 1958, although 15 Silver Wraiths were sold in 1959. Among these was a four-door convertible, which went to Haile Selassie, Emperor of Ethiopia. King Paul of Greece ordered an identical model, as did the government of Australia. Two long-wheelbase Park Ward limousines were sold to British embassies in Copenhagen and Rio de Janeiro.

LEFT • Hooper built this 1956 Sports Saloon body on a Silver Cloud I chassis. The sweeping fender line mimics Hooper's traditional side treatment.

BELOW • This more conservative 1955 Silver Cloud I Sedan accents the subtle treatments Hooper put into its designs, as above.

THE SILVER CLOUD

Rolls-Royce replaced the Silver Dawn with the Silver Cloud, introduced in April 1955. As with all Rolls-Royce models in the past, the Silver Cloud was built with a separate body and chassis, allowing buyers the option to have a custom body rebuilt on the chassis. About 10 percent of buyers opted for custom bodies by Hooper, James Young, or H. J. Mulliner. Mulliner built a two-door, four-seat cabriolet, while the owner of a chain of German department stores ordered a two-door coupe. In addition, several were built with station-wagon bodies. Freestone & Webb built three two-passenger convertibles with tail fins, which were nicknamed "Honeymoon Express."

Contemporary with the Bentley S1, the Silver Cloud was offered in two wheelbase lengths, 123 and 127 inches. The car used a frame of new design, with box-section cross members and a central X-bracing. The independent front suspension consisted of triangular upper and lower control arms (double wishbones), coil springs, and a stabilizer bar. The rear suspension used leaf springs. While there were hydraulic shock absorbers at all four corners, only the rears were electrically adjustable.

Under the hood was the F-head six carried over from the Silver Wraith but with a rebored block to yield 4,887 cc. SU carburetors replaced the single Stromberg or Zenith used on earlier engines. Horsepower was listed as "sufficient." A top speed of 100 mph was possible, making the Silver Cloud the first Rolls-Royce to reach that figure officially. Zero-to-60 mph times were in the neighborhood of 13 seconds, reasonable for a car that weighed more than two tons.

Power steering and air conditioning became options on Rolls-Royce cars in 1956. On long-wheelbase models after that date they were standard equipment.

The last Silver Cloud was delivered in August 1959. It was also the last Rolls-Royce six-cylinder model. When you consider that Henry Royce had designed the original six-cylinder engine in 1922 and used it in the Twenty, the company got its

CLOUD II FACTS

Rolls-Royce built 2,417 short-wheelbase Silver Cloud II models and 299 with the long wheelbase. Mulliner built 107 convertibles on the short-wheelbase chassis and two on the longer wheelbase. Most of the long-wheelbase chassis for both were fitted with bodies by James Young.

Comparisons between a 1961 Mulliner cabriolet and a 1959 Park Ward convertible show two distinctly different cars. The newer car shows a classic profile with a kick-up in front of the rear wheel arch and a gracefully dipping fender line from the center of the rear wheel arch backward. The older car is more slab-sided, with no character lines. Mulliner's car had two headlights, Park Ward's four.

money's worth out of the design. Rolls-Royce built 2,238 short-wheelbase Silver Clouds and 121 with the long wheelbase.

When you have a good name going for you, why change it? Rolls-Royce obviously felt that way when they came out with the Silver Cloud II in 1959 to replace the Silver Cloud, "posthumously" renamed Silver Cloud I. But the Silver Cloud II was more than just a second edition of the same car. It was a totally new vehicle.

For starters, the Silver Cloud II had a V-8 engine as a powerplant. This was a 90° V with oversquare cylinder dimensions that totaled out at 6,230 cc. With a compression ratio of 8.0:1, it delivered approximately 200 horsepower. This was an engine as only Rolls-Royce could build an engine. The camshafts were gear-driven and ran through an oil bath in each revolution. The cam actuated overhead intake and exhaust valves in an aluminum head, while the pistons traveled in an aluminum block with cast-iron cylinder liners.

A General Motors/Rolls-Royce four-speed Hydra-Matic automatic transmission with a column-mounted shifter was standard.

The frame, steering, and brakes were the same as on the Silver Cloud I. The short-wheelbase version had 123 inches between the wheel centers, while the long-wheelbase version added an extra four inches to that number. On the long-wheelbase version an electrically operated partition between driver and passenger was also supplied. Both rode on 8.20-15-inch tires.

Power steering was standard, but central chassis lubrication disappeared. Most of the grease points were now sealed for life, and the few that remained required maintenance only every 10,000 miles.

Exterior design was similar to the predecessor. Inside, the instrument panel consisted of centrally

located dials, gauges, and switches. A new ventilation system had outlets on the right and left of the dash, and full climate control was optional at extra cost. Leather upholstery, however, was standard on the reclining front seats with their center armrests.

The Silver Cloud III, introduced in 1962 and built for four years, was the last car Rolls-Royce would build with a separate chassis and body. Future Rolls-Royce models, beginning with the Silver Shadow in 1965, would be of unibody construction.

The Silver Cloud III faced formidable challengers in the marketplace. Besides the Cadillacs and Lincolns that Rolls-Royce competed with in the United States, Mercedes-Benz introduced the 600 in September 1963. But, over the course of their manufacturing runs, Mercedes-Benz sold 2,677 cars in 18 years. Rolls-Royce sold 2,376 Silver Cloud IIIs in four years, and added 1,630 Bentleys that were essentially identical.

The engine was the same 6,230-cc V-8 that gained approximately 8 percent in power, to about 216 horsepower. This increase was due to a larger carburetor and new piston design.

Rolls-Royce continued to use hydraulic drum brakes with two master cylinders and two separate circuits. They were, of course, power-assisted.

Standard equipment included power steering and a three-speed automatic transmission, the same GM/Rolls-Royce Hydra-Matic. Quad headlights were now standard.

Rolls built 2,044 short-wheelbase (123 inches) vehicles and 253 long-wheelbase (127 inches) versions. Seventy-nine of the long-wheelbase cars were built with special coachwork, usually by James Young. Among these were two two-door designs that were sold to King Hassan II of Morocco.

CLOCKWISE FROM TOP LEFT: **Rolls-Royce also built a Continental version of the Silver Cloud Convertible.**

A 1961 long-wheelbase version of the silver Cloud II was also available, stretching the chassis four inches.

The Silver Cloud III, introduced in 1962, was the last Rolls-Royce built with a separate chassis and body. This convertible opened new markets for the company.

With exterior design similar to its predecessor, the 1960 Silver Cloud II concealed an all-new 6.2-liter V-8 engine under the hood that was capable of 200 hp.

CLOCKWISE FROM TOP:
Detail of the Rolls-Royce Dart engines
which powered the Vickers Viscount
turboprop airliner

Passengers in the 1913 Alpine Eagle at
the Austrian Alpine Trials

Detail of the Boeing 747's powerful
RB211 engines

If the Battle of Britain was won by the
British Spitfire over the German
Messerschmitt, it may well have been
because of the Rolls-Royce Merlin and
Griffon engines powering them.

DESPITE ITS AMAZING AUTOMOBILES AND THE

WONDERFUL HISTORY THEY HAVE ENJOYED,

ROLLS-ROYCE IN THE LAST YEARS OF THE

TWENTIETH CENTURY HAS BEEN PRIMARILY A

JET-ENGINE MANUFACTURER. THE AUTOMOBILES

ARE SECONDARY.

ROLLS-ROYCE BEGAN BUILDING AIRCRAFT ENGINES

DURING WORLD WAR I. HENRY ROYCE WAS INITIALLY

RELUCTANT TO COMMENCE DESIGN OF A NEW

ENGINE, BUT NATIONAL PRIDE AND THE URGING OF

CLAUDE JOHNSON OVERCAME THAT RELUCTANCE,

AND HE BEGAN WORKING ON ONE. ROYCE BEGAN IN

1915 BY STUDYING RENAULT AND MERCEDES RACING

ENGINES. HE GAINED INSPIRATION FROM BOTH OF

THESE. HIS FIRST AIRPLANE ENGINE WAS A V-12

CONFIGURATION, CALLED THE "EAGLE."

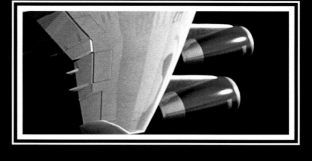
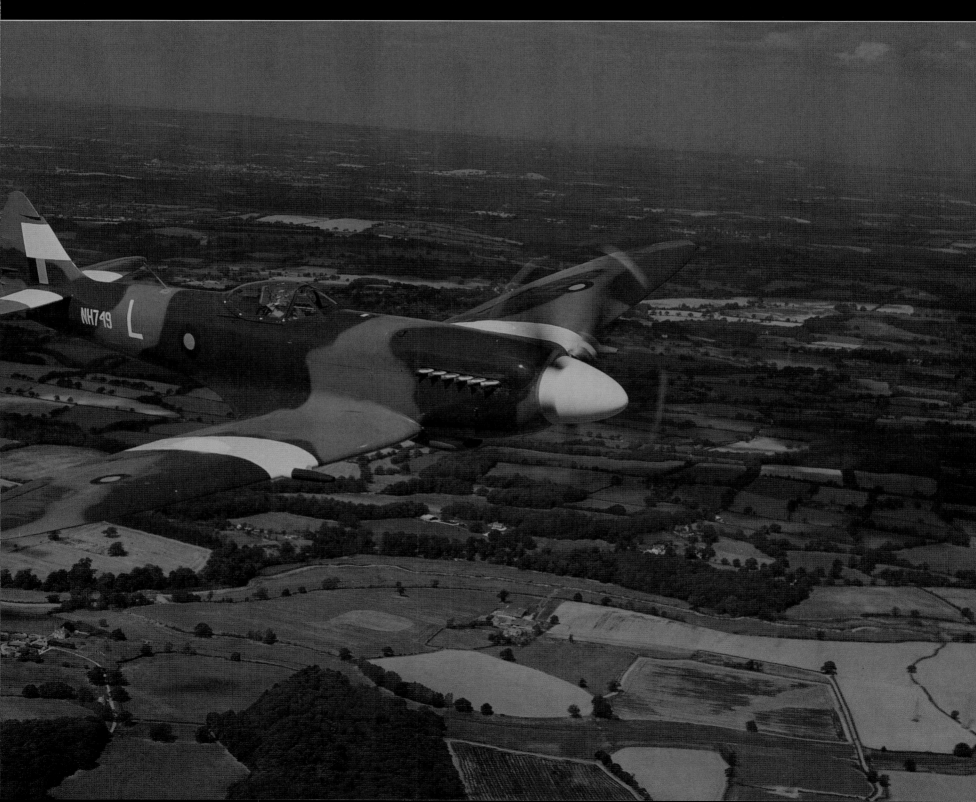

Eagle first ran in October 1915 at Derby and produced 225 horsepower at 1,800 rpm. In less than three years, the power had improved to 360 horsepower. The Rolls-Royce engine powered the first airplane to cross the Atlantic Ocean in June 1919 in a Vickers-Vimy biplane piloted by Alcock and Brown.

Three other Royce airplane engines were the 285-horsepower Falcon, the 100-horsepower Hawk for airships, and the 600-horsepower Condor.

Rolls-Royce engines won the Schneider Trophy for racing seaplanes in 1929 and 1931. In the Supermarine S6 and S6B, Rolls-Royce won the trophy and established a new world air-speed record of more than 400 mph in 1931. Rolls-Royce would go on to establish new world speed records on land and water.

Some historians claim the Battle of Britain was not between Spitfires and Hurricanes on the British side and Messerschmitt 109s and 110s on the German side, but between Rolls-Royce engines and Mercedes-Benz engines fitted in the aeroplanes.

Success in World War II transformed Rolls-Royce from a relatively small company into a major contender in aeropropulsion. At one time, more than half the aircraft engines in the world were designed and manufactured by Rolls-Royce.

During World War II, Rolls-Royce began developing the aero gas-turbine engine pioneered by Sir Frank Whittle. The Welland engine entered military service in the Gloster Meteor fighter plane in 1944. A new world speed record was established by the Meteor using the more powerful Derwent engine. With this kind of success, Rolls-Royce stopped work on piston airplane engines and concentrated on the gas turbine, since it had the lead in that technology. Military jets from many countries used Rolls-Royce engines. In 1953, the Vickers Viscount with a Dart prop-jet engine was Rolls-Royce's first entry in the civil-aviation market.

Between the two World Wars, the major manufacturers of air engines in Europe were Armstrong Siddeley, Blackburn, Bristol, de Havilland, and Napier. Bristol was the leader and merged with Armstrong Siddeley in 1959. Bristol Siddeley and Rolls-Royce absorbed the three other small companies in 1961. Rolls-Royce and Bristol merged in 1966. Bristol Siddeley engines powered the Harrier jump jet and the SST Concorde, among others.

MOVING APART...

In the late 1960s, Rolls Royce introduced the RB211 for the Lockheed L1011 TriStar. Because of early problems with this engine, the company was taken into state ownership and the motorcar business was separated. Eventually, the RB211 established itself as a world-class family of engines, and powers the L1011, Boeing 747, 757, and 767, and the Tupolev TU204.

Rolls-Royce plc returned to the private sector and consolidated its capabilities in the industrial sector. The company expanded its presence in the aeropropulsion field with the acquisition of the Allison Engine Company of the United States in 1995.

Rolls-Royce does not have an outstanding competition heritage. Ferrari, Europe's other most famous small-volume producer, uses its competition heritage to help sell road cars. Rolls-Royce has no such heritage.

Yet, from the days of Charles Rolls and the Tourist Trophy, Rolls-Royce cars have not shied away from competition. The company chose endurance trials

BELOW • **Boeing Aviation uses four Rolls-Royce RB211 engines on its 747 airliner. This engine is also used on the Boeing 757 and 767, as well as the Lockheed L1011 and Tupelev TU204.**

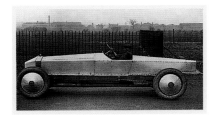

rather than out-and-out racing events to promote its products. Claude Johnson, for one, drove a 30-horsepower model in the 1906 Scottish trials, a 1,000-mile event. Rolls-Royce at one time held the record for the run from Monte Carlo to London.

In 1907, a 40/50 model covered 2,000 miles on British roads using only the top gear. Then the same car went on a nonstop run between London and Glasgow with Claude Johnson, Eric Platford, Charles Rolls, and a driver named Macready driving. The car covered 15,000 miles driving back and forth, resting only on Sundays. At the end of the marathon journey the car only required minor repairs.

Two other 40/50 models were prepared for reliability trials. Named Silver Knight and Silent Rogue, they had engine modifications that increased the output to 70 horsepower. They drove an honest 70 mph on the new Brooklands race track. Ernest Hives drove a Silver Ghost with special bodywork at Brooklands in 1911 and reached a speed of 100 mph.

When a private entrant, James Radley, was disqualified from the 1912 Austrian Alpine Trial for stalling his Silver Ghost on the Katchburg Pass and failing to restart, Rolls-Royce took umbrage. The following year the company prepared four cars with improved engines and new four-speed gearboxes. This time Radley dominated the event from start to finish and won at a speed of 81.93 mph. He won again in 1914 and was the only competitor to complete the run with no penalty points. Rolls-Royce celebrated the victories with a small run of "Alpine Eagles" with special bodywork.

Bentley was the prime race car from Derby and Crewe for several years, but Rolls-Royce owners and drivers could occasionally be seen in competition. A Silver Shadow and Silver Cloud III took part in the World Cup Rally to Mexico in 1970.

BELOW • The 1913 Rolls-Royce Alpine Eagle was a sporting version of the Silver Ghost, name for the Rolls-Royce sweep of the 1913 Austrian Alpine Trials.

BOTTOM • The 1913 Alpine Eagle used a six-cylinder 7.4-liter engine that would move the vehicle to 82 mph. It was the Rolls-Royce's reliability that helped it win the trial, though.

THE WEIRD AND THE WONDERFUL

Outside the competition arena there have been other unique Rolls-Royce models. Custom coachbuilders build Sedanca de Villes and Roi des Belges and cabriolet bodies on all manner of Rolls-Royce chassis. Occasionally, an owner would want something more, and there are any number of Rolls-Royce "shooting brakes" in the world. These are elegant station wagons, often used for hunting and often simply as any other station wagon, but with infinitely more class.

One American owner modified his Rolls-Royce after the back end of his car was destroyed in an accident. He converted it to a pickup truck for a truly different type of utility. Yet, some Rolls-Royce models achieve their notoriety through other circumstances, particularly when involved with the rich and famous.

When fabulous wealth enabled the Beatle John Lennon to afford a Rolls-Royce, he bought one, then painted it yellow with psychedelic designs all over it. In Oregon, Bhagwan Shree Rajneesh ran a commune. His success at raising money, either from his devotees or through other means, enabled him to amass a fleet of 84 Rolls-Royces. Many of these cars were used as rolling canvasses by one of his disciples, Swami Deva Peter, who painted 64 white cranes on one black sedan, peacocks along the side of another, a kimono on a third, rainbows, clouds, prisms, sunrise, and sunsets, flames and waves on some of the Bhagwan's cars.

TOP LEFT • With its wooden body aft of the cowl, the 1926 20 hp Rolls-Royce shooting brake resembled an American 1950s "Woody" station wagon.

TOP RIGHT • Some owners had "shooting brake" bodies constructed on Rolls-Royce chassis. This 1926 20 hp model was used to transport the owner's hunting dogs.

9

THE SWEET & BITTER YEARS

CLOCKWISE FROM TOP:
Wheel arch detail of the Rolls-Royce
Corniche III.

Wheel arch detail of the sporty yet
solid Camargue.

The Rolls-Royce Corniche II.

1988 Silver Spirit grille detail.

THE CAR MAKERS OF ROLLS-ROYCE HAVE OVERCOME MANY PROBLEMS—EVEN CRISES—OVER THE YEARS, NOT LEAST OF WHICH WAS THE 1971 BANKRUPTCY OF THE PARENT AERO-ENGINE COMPANY. THE GROUP WAS BROUGHT DOWN BY UNDERESTIMATING THE PRODUCTION COSTS FOR THE RB211, A NEW-TECHNOLOGY ENGINE FOR THE LOCKHEED L1011 TRISTAR. IT WAS AKIN TO THE BRITISH ROYAL FAMILY SELLING OFF BUCKINGHAM PALACE FOR CONVERSION INTO UPMARKET APARTMENTS. ROLLS-ROYCE, MAKERS OF WHAT WERE PROCLAIMED TO BE THE WORLD'S FINEST MOTORCARS AND JET ENGINES, WAS THE PRIDE OF BRITAIN—A SYMBOL OF EXCELLENCE. IT WAS LIKE THE BANK OF ENGLAND GOING BUST.

ABOVE • **The Silver Shadow, introduced in 1965, amounted almost to a technical revolution by Rolls-Royce standards. It was the first to have a monocoque steel body shell and independent suspension, with automatic height control, and four wheel disk breaking.**

The Receiver, Rupert Nicholson, produced a skilled survival plan—selling the aerospace assets to the British government, and spinning off the car division into a separate company. It was a narrow squeak for the makers of a car that was still revered internationally as a benchmark by which quality was judged. Rolls-Royce Motors, as it is renamed, prospered in its new independence, building upon the Silver Shadow sedan series it had launched six years earlier. It developed a convertible at its Mulliner Park Ward coachbuilding works in London, and many niche models over the following 27 years, showing more adventurousness and ingenuity than any management had dared try in the old days. They hated the words "special edition" but that was the business the company took on. It was realized that the sort of people who can afford astronomical sums for a luxury car also want it to be different from the one owned by the rich guy next door. The American market was the target, and many special features were crafted and engineered into the basic cars to add pizzazz and, to use a polite Rollsy term, "considerably elevate the tariff."

But the road was a rocky one at times. The fierce recession of the early nineties was the catalyst that devastated Rolls-Royce, almost dispatching the venerable car maker to the great metal scrapyard in space where Packard, Pierce Arrow, and other distinguished names probably wound up.

Rolls-Royce, like the other very highly priced cars in the exotic league, Ferrari and Lamborghini, had never really been affected by recession. There had been a few blips along the way, but nothing to dilute the wine list from Veuve Clicquot to a cheap red on the left bank. As the eighties finished, the company just was not prepared for the big one. Production and sales were running at record levels, profits were good—then the roof fell in! Within months of hitting a record—3,333 sales worldwide in 1990—the market almost evaporated. Sales nose-dived 48 percent in the year to 1,722, then down to 1,378 the following year, and to 1,360 in 1993. In North America, the most important overseas market, the fall was even steeper—from nearly 1,200 in 1990 to 408.

The worldwide recession had finally caught up with the normally insulated—the company and its buyers. Many Rolls-Royce and Bentley owners are self-made millionaires, but it dawned upon even the most insensitive among them that conspicuous consumption is out when you're firing people and closing plants.

And when you're fighting to save your business, as many were in this severe and prolonged economic downturn, going out to pay ten times an average yearly income for a luxury car could not be at the forefront of one's thinking.

History demonstrated that Rolls-Royce was virtually bulletproof. Within the company and its dealers in Britain where car selling had been raised to a loftiness matched only in London's exclusive private banks, there was a comfort level in the psyche—the world would wait however long, pay whatever price, and line up for the car. In the 1970s, in fact, dealers would not hand over your new Rolls unless you traded in the old one. Some people ordered a new one every year, which, considering its quality and longevity factor, was rather like saying, "I change it when the ashtrays are full!"

The solid customer base, continually being added to as the nouveau riche expanded, led to complacency. The company, making a virtue of antiquity, had never claimed to be on the leading edge of automotive technology. Change was slow. Without a 50,000-mile road test, a new component wouldn't be considered.

Much is to be said for the American philosophy, "if it ain't broke, don't fix it," and for the wisdom of keeping well-proven components that do the job well. But the automotive industry has made technological strides at an unprecedented pace in the past 20 years. Rolls-Royce was not in the vanguard. True, most owners disliked the idea of "model years" or significant changes.

British owners were comfortable with their motorcars, and forgave not having the latest gizmo, but dealers and owners in North America, where driving a car as technically advanced as Mercedes or BMW was commonplace, were vocal in their demand that Rolls-Royce stay current. Several years after Lexus emerged with a steering wheel that conveniently slid away from the driver when the ignition key was removed, Rolls-

Royce still did not have one. The absence of even a ho-hum telescopic/tilt steering column found on many lesser cars was defended by pointing out that the driver's seat had six positions of adjustment, thereby making a movable steering column unnecessary. And there were devout persuaders at Crewe who believed that.

The real problem was economic, allied to a traditional reluctance to continue changing things. Rolls-Royce, a small company producing small numbers of cars—each one taking three or more months to build—could not afford to change anything very often. A body style had to last many years because the cost of retooling and altering the shape was prohibitive when, necessarily, it had to be amortized over a tiny output. Radical improvements to match other luxury-car makers just could not be financed. Certainly, new components were bought in, but Rolls was to a considerable extent a prisoner of both old technology and complicated, time-consuming ways of doing things. It was easier said than done to accommodate a new, updated piece. Many technical changes of course had to be incorporated to freshen the cars, and occasionally a quantum leap forward, as in the case of the computer-controlled adaptive suspension in 1989, which gave the range of heavy saloons—never previously noted for their wondrous handling characteristics—the cornering attributes of a sports car.

ABOVE • **The Silver Shadow became one of Rolls-Royce's most successful models. The convertible shown here was produced in 1972.**

TOP • **Regarded by many as the most beautiful Rolls-Royce ever built, the Corniche convertible has become a classic. Hand-crafted by master coachbuilders at the Mulliner Park Ward works, the body took several weeks to shape before being taken to Crewe for mechanical fitments, then being returned to MPW for interior furnishing and the top.**

ABOVE • **The beautiful Bentley T-Type Corniche.**

The Silver Shadow, launched in 1965, represented radical change in Rolls-Royce car design and engineering. The marque's first monocoque body of steel integral construction, with hood, trunk lid, and doors made of aluminum alloy, it had no traditional separate chassis frame, the stress being taken by a single skin. Reaction to it was mixed. The purists, thinking of the Silver Cloud, thought the Shadow inelegant and too boxy.

The objective was to build a lower and more compact car than the Cloud, but with more room inside. The company proudly listed its technical attributes. It was the first Rolls-Royce to have a self-leveling, independent, front and rear suspension, and backup braking system. The automatic transmission was fitted with a unique electric-gear-range selector. Over the next 12 years, 2,000 modifications and improvements would be engineered into this model, along with its siblings—the long-wheelbase Shadow and two-door hardtop and convertible models. All told, 20,594 were built.

They included Bentley versions, the Bentley T series, the only difference from a Rolls-Royce being the grille and badging. Also in the range, the Rolls-Royce Corniche convertible launched just weeks after the 1971 receivership. This beautiful coachbuilt car, along with a coupe version, crafted by hand at the Mulliner Park Ward works in West London, was and is still regarded as one of the most desirable Rolls-Royce classics. The Corniche shared most mechanical components with the Shadow, but was different in many respects. The body shell was shaped by craftsmen at Mulliner, transported 200 miles or so to the Crewe factory where the hardware was installed, then returned to London for skilled artisans to perform their magic—the crafting of flawless panel veneers, Connolly leather upholstery, Wilton and lambswool rugs. It was an expensive and time-consuming process, almost six months being required for the completion of each car. It took one man a week, for example, to fit the convertible top—a work of such

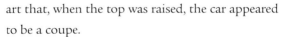

art that, when the top was raised, the car appeared to be a coupe.

The Silver Shadow II made its bow in 1977, with a long-wheelbase version that was now given a name, the Silver Wraith II. This had four inches more leg room in the rear passenger compartment, a discreet smaller rear window, and, if you really wanted privacy, an electrically powered division to shut off the front seats.

The Camargue (codenamed Delta during development), often described as the rarest Rolls-Royce, took its name from the area roamed by wild horses in Southern France. The impressive, two-door coachbuilt coupe owed its existence to David Plastow, the company's chief executive, who pushed for a different type of Rolls. At the 1976 introduction—where the $90,000 price dazzled the American media—the car was said by Rolls-Royce to have been developed over a five-year period to meet the requirements of owners who preferred to drive themselves, and wanted a motorcar combining traditional Rolls-Royce qualities with hand-built, stylish, and exclusive coachwork. Rolls turned to

the noted Italian designer Sergio Pininfarina for the styling, which included jutting the radiator shell forward of its base—a radical departure! Built on the basic Silver Shadow/Corniche platform, it was crafted at Mulliner Park Ward. Its four-wheel disc brakes were actuated by three separate hydraulic systems. Eight and a half inches wider than the Corniche, the Camargue offered space, as the publicity people pointed out, for "an extra golf bag or two in the enlarged luggage compartment." It was certainly a different-looking Rolls—very wide—and with huge heavy doors. One journalist said, "Not good Rolls-Royce—not good Pininfarina." But it had its fans, and engineers at the factory claimed it to be the best riding car the company had ever produced. Over its 11-year production life, 534 were built.

The Camargue "close-out" in 1986 was a good example of the marketing spin practiced by the American subsidiary Rolls-Royce Motor Cars, Inc. Camargues, it was said, had been used as personal transportation by kings, princes, diplomats, and captains of industry around the world. Now, the final 25 would be a limited

TOP LEFT • The Camargue, designed by Pininfarina, was a huge, heavy two-door, described as "a coupe of understated elegance."

TOP • Based on the Silver Shadow platform, the stylish Corniche Saloon was introduced as the Mulliner Park Ward two-door saloon. This was later to become the Corniche coupe.

MIDDLE • A classic look to the 1977 Silver Shadow II, embodying elegance and style.

BOTTOM • The solid, powerful Camargue appealed to the sportier Rolls-Royce owner. A limited production car, only 534 were made, the Camargue's value soared on the used car market.

edition to commemorate the 80th anniversary of the first sale of a Rolls-Royce in America. The specification was special—and so was the price at $175,000. Features included veneers with silver inlays, a phone, monogrammed silver-plated cocktail flasks, crystal glasses, a vanity set, leather attaché case, and a silver pen and notepad. All were in white with red upholstery—and they became collectors' models, within a few years fetching almost $100,000 over the close-out price. What price, I wonder, for the one Camargue built as a Bentley model? That would be a collector's item.

The last of the great Rolls-Royce carriages was the seven-seat Phantom VI limousine—one of which was purchased by the British motor industry to present to Queen Elizabeth on her jubilee in 1977. A fraction under 20 feet long, stylish and elegant, the PVI was majestic and a classic—everyone's idea of a true Rolls-

Royce. It took the Mulliner Park Ward craftsmen about 14 months to put one together, starting with a steel chassis of strength and weight that would have done justice to a London bus or a Vickers tank. The body was formed over an inner cage of corrosion-protected steel and wood, to which a skin of aluminum panels was fitted. Up to 18 cows gave their all for the upholstery, their full-thickness hides being tailored by hand. The woodwork, of course, was of figured, burled, Lombardian walnut. Old-fashioned wringing-machine-like rollers were used to shape the metal and give the limousine its glorious sweeping coachlines. And, when it was time to make the roof, a dozen burly men hoisted a huge flat piece of steel atop the framework, and began to shape the roof from there. The rear compartment had two foldaway occasional seats the size of small easy chairs, and motors to lift the rear seats to ensure that the occupants could be seen by mortals outside. The Phantom VI represented everything that was luxurious, solid, and durable about Rolls-Royce.

INNOVATION PAYS OFF

These models were big improvements over the original Shadows, incorporating powered rack-and-pinion steering, gas springs in a new rear suspension to adjust the ride to the load and improve cornering, and the unique Rolls-Royce dual-level automatic air conditioning introduced the previous year in the two-door Camargue. This highly sophisticated system assured occupants of "warm toes and a cool head" and, it was claimed, once set, required no further adjustment whether you were in the desert or driving from Anchorage to Arizona. The odometer was designed to record

journeys up to one million miles, and the famous ticking clock was finally banished, giving way to a silent electronic digital display.

The Shadow/Wraith Mark IIs were great money spinners, and squeezed an extra four years of life from the design, giving more breathing space to prepare the Silver Spirit and Silver Spur models. Eight and a half thousand Shadow IIs were built and 2,134 Wraith IIs—this model selling well in the United States, where buyers preferred the extra room over the short wheelbase. An additional 560 were built with Bentley grilles.

But this was no Ferrari. This huge, gleaming vehicle—like a 747 sans wings—rightly occupied pole position at the very pinnacle of powered ground transportation. Skill was required to handle her—a definite need here for a brawny chauffeur. It was rather like steering the *Queen Elizabeth II* or a well-upholstered oil tanker. You stared well ahead and anticipated braking requirements before other drivers would even think about it. Like its predecessors, the Phantom handled something like a truck, and the brakes always had plenty on to bring it to a halt if the driver had pressed the pedal to the metal and worked up some impetus. The engineers would grin and tell you, "In one of these, you can drive right through a Japanese car without spilling your drink."

ENTER THE SPIRIT AND THE SPUR

There was little doubt that the Silver Shadow was suffering styling fatigue toward the end of its run. Rolls aficionados in 1980 certainly welcomed the Silver Spirit and long-wheelbase Silver Spur, the first new production models in 15 years.

SZ, as the model was codenamed, had taken eight years to develop. Rolls had changed—but had it? The rest of the world was actively designing and building lighter, more fuel-efficient cars. There had been a major fuel crisis in 1977, but Rolls-Royce continued developing its new cars, unable at that stage to take much weight out, and saddled still with the old aluminum-alloy, 6.75 liter, V-8 engine—larger than anything else on the road. And each year the company successfully sought exemption from US milage requirements on the grounds it was a small manufacturer, and meeting increasingly stringent standards was technically and financially impossible. "To get a good ride you need a big solid car, and if it's a gas guzzler so be it." The new cars emerged just as big, heavy, and thirsty as their predecessors.

The interior had been redesigned with an attractive new instrument panel. Three inches wider and an inch lower than their predecessors, the aim was to make the Spirit and Spur contemporary and aerodynamically efficient, yet retain sophisticated Rolls-Royce elegance. The proclaimed goal of better aerodynamics was stretching it a bit, but the windscreen was more sharply raked and there was 30 percent more glass area. Technical improvements included rack-and-pinion steering, self-leveling suspension, and an electronic odometer. The split-level air conditioning, it was claimed, had the heating capacity of four radiators and cooling power of 30 refrigerators.

A sensor near the windshield even helped the air conditioner to compensate for heat generated by sunlight. The publicists drew attention to the pin-tumbler door locks, patterned after one designed in Egypt 4,000 years previously to protect the tomb of a pharaoh. The odds against a thief successfully forging a key was claimed to be 24,000 to one. And for good measure, a transmission lock automatically activated when the ignition key was removed.

The Silver Spur was described as "eminently suitable for formal business use with a chauffeur, or for the enjoyment of the owner who wished to drive himself." The car, claimed the company, combined advanced engineering with graceful lines and luxurious appointments.

TOP LEFT • 1989 Silver Spur. Although the shape was new, many mechanical features were carried over from the SY Shadow series.

TOP • 1988 Silver Spirit engine. The company was so sure of it the odometer was designed, as with the Silver Shadow II, to record journeys up to one million miles.

BOTTOM • The interior of the 1988 Silver Spirit shows the luxurious cabin with classic instrument panel and awash with leather.

ABOVE • **An example of badge engineering, the Mulsanne was a Silver Shadow with a Bentley grille—hailed as "the return of the silent sports car". A later turbo-charged version, with electrifying performance, paved the way to place the Bentley marque as the company's sporting and performance product.**

The Bentley version was the Mulsanne, named after a straight on the Le Mans circuit where Bentleys achieved so many racing triumphs. "The return of the silent sports car" was the theme—"a fast sporting machine—the latest statement of the Bentley philosophy." Rolls saw the Mulsanne as a performance saloon of impeccable road manners, fastidious attention to detail, silence, and comfort, coming together in the newest of an elegant line of fine motorcars that had made Bentley a byword among enthusiasts for more than half a century.

But it was a Rolls under the skin—again, the only difference being the grille and badging.

The Mulsanne Turbo was an instant success, drivers marveling at the aircraft-like way its speed was unleashed without signs of the engine working hard. But there was one problem. With ride comfort a major objective, the suspension was not uprated, and would-be Nigel Mansells had to exercise caution to avoid taking the chrome off the door handles or winding up crashing through a fence on the Watford bypass. Then along came Michael Dunn, a brilliant engineer with a track record at Ford. He became Rolls-Royce director of engineering, and injected urgent purpose into

engineering development. Something had to be done about the Mulsanne Turbo's handling.

The challenge was to add to a suspension system that had changed little in concept for nearly 20 years, to tighten the handling yet retain ride quality, and match or beat the best of competitive luxury cars. Front and rear damping resistance and roll-bar rates were increased under the direction of the vehicle chief engineer, Phil Harding, and new wide alloy wheels to take Pirelli P7 tires were designed and produced at Crewe.

Steering was stiffened, and, with a new airdam to help stability and some additional suspension tweaks, the Mulsanne Turbo was transformed into an impressive performance car—docile in the town, but able to blow the doors off a BMW or a Porsche on the open road.

With the arrival in 1993 of Peter Ward as new marketing chief (later to become chairman and chief executive), Michael Dunn found a soul mate who wanted to reinvent Bentley, and widen the product and customer base by giving motorists a choice. The prestigious Rolls-Royce would be there for those desiring luxury—the Bentley for more sporting and adventurous drivers.

TOP • The Turbo R was refined and performance-tweaked to the point where some suggested Rolls-Royce should make applicants take a driving competence test before being permitted to buy one.

MIDDLE • The command post. The luxurious front compartment of the flagship Bentley Turbo R fitted with analog instrumentation and the finest leather and veneer.

BOTTOM • The two and a half ton Bentley Turbo R, known as "Crewe's Missile", astonished the motoring world with a zero to sixty acceleration time of 6.5 seconds.

ENTER THE BENTLEYS

Until 1982, that is, when the first move was made to distance Bentley from Rolls-Royce—and really offer a driver a choice of more substance than badging. The Bentley Mulsanne Turbo was launched for Britain and Europe (its engine would not get through the tough emission tests in the United States). With startling acceleration— 0–60 in 7 seconds, and a top speed of 134 mph, the Mulsanne was transformed into a luxury express by a Garrett single-exhaust-driven turbocharger. Rolls modified its famous coyness about its cars' performance— always described as "adequate"—when it publicly opined with a wry smile, "The Mulsanne Turbo's performance is adequate, plus 50 per cent!"

But for those who put sportiness above luxury a less expensive Bentley was quickly cobbled together. The Bentley Eight was produced in 1984 to attract entry-level buyers. It bore a wire-mesh grille, reminiscent of the Bentley Boys' glory days at Le Mans; it didn't have the Turbo performance, and lacked a few of the top-of-the line refinements, like patterned walnut, but it was sporty and more affordable, and it got you into the club.

The following year a stellar product—the Turbo R— launched as the ultimate luxury sporting four-door saloon. Peter Ward's zeal for a great driving car, and Michael Dunn's leadership of the engineering department (see box), had turned the Mulsanne Turbo into a faster, more responsive road warrior with powerful brakes, a cockpit-like interior, sports-style seats, and comprehensive instrumentation cosseted in the richest burl walnut.

Within months, the commitment to develop a separate Bentley range, markedly different from the cars bearing a Rolls-Royce grille, was underscored by the

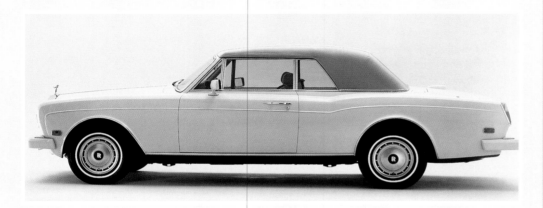

The art of the coachbuilder is exemplified in the Rolls-Royce Corniche III, an elegant convertible which combined graceful styling with almost decadent luxury. The finest materials were reserved for the Corniche III, especially the leather seating and veneer paneling, offering the ultimate in top-down touring. The construction of the top alone required a full week's work by one craftsman. In the up position, it fits so perfectly, the car looks like a hardtop coupe.

return of a great name, the Bentley Continental—a stylish sister convertible to the Corniche. This was described as a classic luxury sporting convertible, offering the best of two worlds—the exhilaration of top-down motoring in the grand manner with sports-style seats, and the advantage of a quiet coupé when the weather was less than kind.

The Corniche also was being refined. The Rolls-Royce Corniche II went into production in 1987—for US buyers only in the first year—in response to the American marketing arm's pleas for a more interesting product. Two years later, a Corniche III emerged with a more exclusive (in terms of numbers) Bentley Continental version—models the company said were of timeless elegance. With flawless fit and finish, these beautiful motorcars were striking testimony to the skills of the craftsmen and women at Mulliner Park Ward who sculpted the metal and wood and tailored leather and wool into cars that dreams are made of.

Rolls-Royce minders, meanwhile, had not been idle. Concern about body-shop entrepreneurs in the States cutting Silver Spurs into two, adding a new midsection and calling the result a Rolls-Royce limousine, was increasing at Crewe. The company had no control over

the engineering disciplines applied, commenting that it was a complicated car to slice into, and worried that if one had a collision, and broke into two pieces, the world might think it was a factory-built car. So the decision was taken to fight fire with real fire, and the Silver Spur Limousine was introduced in 1984. Rolls did the cutting itself at Mulliner Park Ward—meticulously adding three feet to the length, and creating a luxurious chariot for the captain of industry or the pop star, complete with TV, VCR, hi-fi, and drinks cabinets. But it looked a bit odd since the extended body was just that—stretched, sausage style. The first 16 to be built had no increase in width or height to keep the vehicle in proportion.

An even longer version, a 42-inch stretch, was produced, based on the Silver Spur II platform, and this did have a raised roof, which made the dimensions more appealing. They didn't talk about these cars back in England where the appearance of one on the streets of London would have been regarded as the height of vulgarity and obviously the property of those dreadful people in Dallas or Beverly Hills. Nonetheless, the Silver Spur limousine presaged the death-knell of the Phantom, being more easily built and more practical for everyday activity.

By now, the company had seen the wisdom of producing "niche" cars to satisfy owners' desires for something different or special. In 1985, Rolls-Royce celebrated the production of its 100,000th car (including Bentleys) with the Silver Spur Centenary. One Centenary car was built, which the company kept, along with 25 replicas.

All the ingenuity and craftsmanship they possessed were crafted into these very special motorcars—many exclusive features like monogrammed waistrails on the

door cappings, inlaid picnic tables and matching spirit flasks, engraved door-sill plates and a commemorative plaque in the glove box. Each car was finished in royal-blue paintwork with the highest-quality champagne-colored hide, and dark-blue carpeting.

The late eighties saw a flurry of model variations—the Corniche III, Silver Spirit II, and Silver Spur II—and an edition by Mulliner Park Ward limited to one hundred was also produced, finished in Bordeaux red with color-matched bumpers and headlight surrounds. Inside were rare "starburst walnut veneers" with silver and boxwood inlays to the fascia, door panels, waistrails, and picnic tables. And of course a cocktail cabinet with a refrigerator in the rear armrest. Also, a humidor compartment, but even cigar lovers conceded that polluting the interior of a Rolls-Royce with cigar smoke was a Philistinian act.

The Bentley market in North America in the mid-to-late eighties was not directly assaulted. It was softened up—prepared over three years—by the entry-level Bentley Eight, the Mulsanne S (a rebadged version of the Mulsanne), and the Continental convertible. The ground was laid for the Turbo R—now qualifying for emissions acceptance, and with automatic ride control, the new computerized suspension that switched instantly from soft to firm, according to how the car was driven. The first six months' Turbo R production was sold in advance.

Three more of the most outstanding Bentley models were on the stocks as financial storm clouds begin to float towards the company.

TOP · **1992 Silver Spirit II**

MIDDLE · **1989 Silver Spur II**

BOTTOM · **To counter "unofficial Rolls-Royce limousines" produced by cutting a car in two and adding a section, Rolls-Royce decided to build its own, introducing a 19 ft 7 in long Touring Limousine, based on the Silver Spur and including picnic tables, television, VCR, and a refrigerator.**

LEFT · **Rolls-Royce capitalized on its heritage by introducing a Bentley version of the Corniche convertible. The classic Bentley Continental added a stylish dimension to the range and widened the customer base. Few were built making each model exclusive.**

10

TOWARD THE NEW MILLENNIUM

CLOCKWISE FROM TOP:
Taillight detail of the stylish and hugely-prized Bentley Continental R, described as the ideal car for the driver who could no longer squeeze into his Porche

Wheel detail of the Rolls-Royce Touring Limousine which could be equipped to become a supremely comfortable mobile living room or office as the owner desired.

Headlight detail of the Bentley Java. Unveiled at the Geneva Motor Show this sleek exciting four-seat roadster with a Cosworth turbo engine received an ecstatic public reaction. However, the concept car was shelved to make way for the Rolls-Royce and Bentley cars of the late nineties.

1992 Rolls-Royce Corniche IV, one of the truly classic Rolls-Royce convertibles of the decade.

THE NINETIES STARTED OFF BITTERSWEET FOR ROLLS. COMING OFF RECORD SALES OF 64 CARS A WEEK IN 1990, THE PLUNGE WAS SUDDEN AND DRAMATIC. THE RECESSION, ALONG WITH AMERICAN BUYERS' REFUSAL TO PAY A NEW LUXURY-CAR TAX, DIDN'T JUST BITE ROLLS-ROYCE ON THE ANKLE. IT AMPUTATED ITS LEGS! A 48 PERCENT PLUNGE TOOK SALES DOWN TO 33 WEEKLY IN 1991, AND 26 CARS IN 1993. ACTION WAS TAKEN—AND FAST.

The company was losing thousands on every car sold. An international consultancy firm was called in to map out a survival plan, and the trauma that engulfed Rolls-Royce was much more devastating than the worries accompanying the bankruptcy 20 years before. Costs had to be cut and more efficient ways found to make the car. One-third of the workforce—1,700—were declared redundant, followed by an additional 950 when further tightening became necessary. The sales collapse, the Gulf War, and economic downturns in major markets, put Rolls seriously into the red. Its parent company, the Vickers Group, also came close to going under.

Restructuring costs at Rolls were more than 31 million pounds in the first year, although critics took the view that the company would have been in better shape to take a hammering had it not been milked for every penny of profit to support Vickers' share price since the merger in 1980.

The cash cow had been starved of needed investment by Vickers, and, in December 1991, Warburg Securities, the international merchant-banking firm, said Rolls-Royce was such a financial drag on Vickers, whose shares were down 40 percent in a year, it should be sold.

Rolls, undergoing two major restructuring campaigns, along with short-time working, was hemorrhaging from every fiscal pore; and, amid increasing speculation that Vickers, too, was bleeding to death, Vickers announced it was reviewing its options. Quietly, Rolls was hawked around. Toyota turned it down when a quick decision was demanded. BMW emerged as a possible buyer but kept on denying it.

ABOVE • **The Bentley Continental R—the first Bentley in 40 years not to share a body-style with a Rolls-Royce, was sleek, very fast, and exclusive, and caught the imagination of the motoring world.**

ABOVE RIGHT • **The Continental R did more to separate Bentley from Rolls-Royce than any other model in the marque. It was unique in the early 90s and was probably the most stylish and desired two-door on the market.**

At Vickers' annual shareholders' meeting, some who had fought in World War II pleaded with the chairman, Sir David Plastow, not to sell to the Germans. He sympathized but pointed out that the board had a duty to shareholders as a whole to realize maximum value from its investments. But he promised no sale before the proposal was put to shareholders.

Plastow was a Rolls man through and through. He had started with the company as a regional sales representative and worked his way up to chief executive of the car division just as the bankruptcy occurred, and later engineered the merger with Vickers. He agonized over selling the company—especially to a German firm. And some believe the high price he demanded of BMW, which caused the Germans to back off, was inflated to achieve just that result. Many would say he was absolutely right, especially six years later, in 1998, several years after David Plastow's retirement, when Vickers made a big profit selling Rolls—ironically to Volkswagen, which came up on the rails to outbid BMW.

BMW's chairman Bernd Pischetsrieder acknowledged in 1994 that he had talked to Vickers about buying Rolls-Royce, and certainly would not exclude the possibility of another approach. The talks foundered, he said, because BMW was willing to pay only one-third the price Plastow had demanded.

DON'T SELL...!

London's Daily Mirror was outraged at the possibility that Rolls could go to BMW, publishing a disparaging leader headed, "hans off." Noting that BMW made cars that companies gave to senior executives who were not worthy of a Mercedes, the paper described Rolls-Royce as a national institution—as British as the bulldog! What the Germans had failed to do to Britain in two World Wars, they might do to its finest cars. It would be a sorry end to cross a bulldog with a dachshund, said the Mirror.

BENTLEY STEALS THE SHOW

Gradually Rolls began to stabilize, but, even as models were freshened and sales improved a little, it continued to struggle. While all this was going on, Bentley stole the 1991 Geneva Motor Show with the surprise unveiling of the Continental R—a stylish two-door, the first Bentley model in 40 years not to share a body shell with a Rolls counterpart. Peter Ward called the coupe a "sporting supercar"—big, comfortable, very powerful, and a motorcar for the connoisseur.

Zero to sixty was covered in 6.6 seconds; top speed was governed electronically to 145 mph (which provoked murmured criticism by road-safety advocates in the US, where there was a national 55 mph limit), and the four-speed automatic transmission could be switched from normal to high-performance at the touch of a switch. The Bentley radiator grille was restyled and tilted back to assist high-speed stability and reduce wind noise.

A sweeping console with a built-in phone extended from the instrument panel to the rear seats, emphasizing the cockpit effect, and, with automatic ride control, antilock brakes, an airbag, heated seats, and a hi-fi system that invited you to sit in the house at night listening to the garage, this most certainly was not your father's Rolls—or even Bentley! "Nepal," as it had been codenamed, was designed by an in-house team led by the chief stylist Graham Hull. They were reinforced by three outside consultants, John Hefferman, Ken Greenley, and Tom Karen. The styling was described by many as breathtaking.

The car was a sensation and Bentley enthusiasts were delirious. There was further intrigue for them in 1993—a new sedan, the Bentley Brooklands, named after the legendary circuit in Surrey where motor

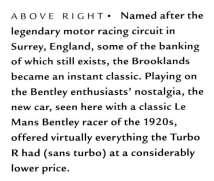

racing was born, and where Walter Bentley himself raced. The Brooklands superseded the Mulsanne. It wasn't turbocharged, but it was luxurious and had sharp performance and all the goodies such as automatic ride control to give it sports-car handling. The Brooklands, along with a long-wheelbase version, developed well in the market, and in the mid-nineties, especially when the performance was enhanced, it took sales away from Turbo R, being seen by buyers as probably the best value offered by the company.

The 1993 model year was a Bentley cavalcade. Six models carried the name—Brooklands standard and with a long wheelbase; the flagship Continental R coupe; Turbo R with a long-wheelbase version; and the Continental convertible. The United States had never seen the Bentley marque represented by such a comprehensive range, and Bentley sales began to overtake Rolls-Royce. Perhaps some buyers had in mind the words murmured by a Bentley fan on a visit to Crewe: "Ah, the Bentley. For the man who has run the race but declines to wear the laurels."

The efficiency measures and the model changes took Rolls-Royce back into profit in 1993, and a major factory-investment program costing 50 million pounds began to bear fruit the following year. The venerable 6.75-liter V-8 engine was partly redesigned, with some of the most significant changes involving alterations to the cylinder heads and air intake, increasing mid-range power by 20 percent.

A new electronic management system, the Bosch M3.3, controlling new direct fuel injection, also reduced exhaust emissions, enabling the entire range to meet worldwide emission requirements. And a leaf was taken from the Germans' book. A neat shroud now covered the engine. No longer could an owner lift the hood and proudly display the magnificent Rolls engine in all its glory. The transmission was also given a new shift-energy-management system which made gear changes even smoother.

The Silver Spur III in 1994, presented as offering unsurpassed comfort and luxury, was joined for the 1995 model year by the Flying Spur—the first turbocharged

CLOCKWISE FROM
TOP LEFT: **1994 Silver Spur**

The fastest Rolls-Royce ever built,
and with a racy title to match—The
Flying Spur was the first Rolls-Royce
to be turbocharged.

The skills of the Mulliner Park Ward
craftsmanship can be seen in the rear
compartment of this special edition
Silver Spur, including picnic tables,
cocktail requisites, and a refrigerator.

Changes inside and out marked the
1996 model year for the Silver Spur
formal saloon—a new center console,
improved ergonomics, and a steering
column which moved away from the
driver when the ignition was off.

THE LITTLE BIG SURPRISE

Bentley Motors, as it's legally called, had another big surprise for the media attending the world's most prestigious automotive event—the Geneva Motor Show—in March 1994. It was a small Bentley, a concept car named Java—with a removable top. The company was careful to stress that the compact was being used to test public reaction, saying cautiously that it was a possible next-generation Bentley. It was a two-door, four-passenger, sporting convertible coupé, with a new twin-turbo V-8 engine designed with the help of Cosworth Engineering, who know a lot about race engines, and it was claimed to be more than a designer's dream car. "We already have the skills and technology to make it a reality," said Michael Donovan, commercial managing director. It could be in production by 2000, and the selling price would be about £90,000.

The car's performance specification was impressive—0–60 mph in 5.6 seconds and 0–100 in 14.2 seconds. And it would do about 30 miles per gallon. It was shown twice more: at the company's Conduit Street showroom in London, and in California at the Pebble Beach Concours—an annual gathering of classic-car enthusiasts noted for their deep pockets. The Tonight talk-show host Jay Leno, an enthusiastic collector, told me he loved it. It was less ostentatious than most Rolls-Bentley products and that would be particularly appealing, he thought, especially in a climate where a well-heeled car owner could come to grief if he encountered the ungodly. Most people enthused about the Java, but the car disappeared, not to be seen again. Development funds were a problem. And even if the cash had been there, updating would have waited until the new millenium. An updated version of the Java could become reality if the new owner, Volkswagen, follows through a plan to build 9,000 Bentleys a year.

Rolls-Royce, which meant it was the fastest Royce ever built. A limited-edition car priced in the US at $225,000, where only 50 were to be marketed, the Flying Spur could hit 60 mph in under seven seconds—quite a performance for a car weighing 5,440 pounds.

The Corniche IV—even more refined by its coachbuilders—appeared along with dual airbags, the passenger-side bag reflecting typical Rolls-Royce commitment to aesthetics. It would have been simple to cover it with leather, but that would have broken the flowing veneer lines of the fascia. The company went to considerable trouble and expense to conceal the airbag behind a veneer-hinged flap where the glove box had been. New lockable stowage space was provided beneath the fascia, which meant removing and redesigning the fuse-box panel that had been in that space. Henry Royce, the man who urged his people to strive for perfection in everything they did, would have been proud. It was a heartwarming reminder that Rolls-Royce continued to try to maintain the standards of excellence laid down by its founders.

The Mulliner Park Ward custom design service was expanded. A "cathedral" devoted to skilled workmanship, available to customers to personalize their motorcars, was created out of an engineering block at Crewe. Here, owners and potential owners could make a pilgrimage to the hallowed factory, wallow in the great range of special features that could be crafted especially for them into their car, and sometimes they would leave ten or twenty thousand pounds the poorer, but richer for their Rolls-Royce. In return, the interior furnishings of the motorcar they would receive would reflect their own personality and taste—provided their instructions did not violate Rolls-Royce Motor Cars' judgment and good taste!

A NEW DAWN...

For the 1995 model year, another saloon car appeared, bringing back a great name—the Silver Dawn. This was unkindly (but with a degree of justification, perhaps) referred to by Rolls watchers as a "cheap Spur." It was an attempt to attract buyers, who found the $169,900 Silver Spur III a bit too rich, to a more affordable version costing a hefty $20,000 less. Some Silver Spur content was removed, including much of the leather. Leather remained on "wearing surfaces" but a "nearly genuine" substitute, a vinyl called Marvellon which looked just like the real thing, was fitted to the sides and behind the seats. The mechanical specification was identical to that of the real Spur, so the buyer was getting a very good performer and in most respects a bargain in Rolls-Royce terms. But the interior fittings fell some way short—not so noticeable if you hadn't examined a Silver Spur III but very evident if you had.

The Mulliner Park Ward artisans stood ready to up the spec—but that would have brought the car into the genuine Silver Spur price range, so why not buy the Spur in the first place? The company rationale, as outlined by the chief executive for the Americas, was that the Silver Dawn made a Rolls-Royce "more reachable" and a realistic alternative to someone who desired to move up from top-of-the-line European cars.

Also produced for 1995—yet another special edition—was a turbocharged Corniche S, another "fastest-ever Rolls-Royce." Twenty would be made, then production of the most glamourous convertible ever built by the company would end. The Corniche had been a great mainstay—a golden goose—over a life spanning a quarter century. But the coachbuilding jigs were old and failing; the price had shot through the roof—it was now $269,000 (plus $24,000 luxury tax, which with state taxes took the price well over $300,000) and demand was falling off. Also, an exciting new Bentley convertible was on the way.

Again Bentley stole the Geneva Show—when it took the wraps off the Azure on March 17, 1995. Orders flowed in for the stunning four-seat turbocharged convertible, which was a joint effort between Gruppo Pininfarina and the stylists and engineers at Crewe. Sergio Pininfarina modestly said, "It is a privilege to combine our world-class skills with those of Rolls-Royce Motor Cars." Those talents had indeed produced a powerful car that was both visually pleasing and

TOP • The most expensive Bentley performance convertible, the Azure was introduced in 1996 in the United States and required more than one third of a million dollars to drive away. They sold out within three weeks.

MIDDLE • A complicated, spectacular hood mechanism turned the Azure into a convertible in seconds.

BOTTOM • The Silver Dawn, reviving a great name, was brought to the market to attract people who could not quite manage the price of the more lavishly equipped Silver Spur.

The Mulliner Park Ward Touring Limousine as the ultimate expression of Rolls-Royce craftmanship. Two feet longer than the Silver Spur, it offers a host of veneer and leather crafted extras, over and above cocktail cabinets, picnic tables, and refrigerators.

technologically advanced. The Azure was designed to capture the essence of grand-touring, "wind-in-the-hair" motoring which appealed to so many Rolls-Royce owners, and, like so many other Rolls-Bentley products, derived its name from the South of France.

One was sent to the United States a few weeks later. The US public-relations arm launched a media blitz in California, Florida, and New York, and even at $319,000—the most expensive car the company had ever offered in North America—the first year's production was sold out within three weeks.

The performance was up there with the other turbo Bentleys—0–60 in seven seconds and a top speed limited to 150 mph. It had automatic ride control, a tilt-steering column (at last) linked to the driver's seat and mirrors, dual-level air conditioning, and two airbags. The four-speed automatic incorporated a shift-energy-management system. Rolls-Royce put every technical attribute it was capable of into the Azure, and it made for a gorgeous, luxurious, dream car that was bound to do wondrous things for the ego.

More changes were made to freshen the remainder of the range for the 1996 model year. The shape the four-door cars had been living with since 1980 was tweaked here and there, a little more rounding going into the styling. The Rolls grille and the Flying Lady were reduced slightly to blend in better, and interiors were given a redesigned look with sweeping new center consoles. The company had sought customer opinion all over the world, and the improvements reflected some of those views. Rear-seat passengers found individual air-conditioning outlets; a new entertainment system was fitted; four-position memory seats for the driver and front passenger were linked to the new tilt-steering wheel; and front headroom was increased by an inch. The seats, too, were more comfortable.

The engine was given new cylinder heads and some other improvements, including the Zytek EMS3 management system, providing smoother and greater acceleration through the speed range. And the company was back in profit. Sales in 1994 reached 1,414, increased to 1,556 in 1995, and went up again in 1996 to 1,744. The climb-back continued in 1997, sales touching 1,918, but faltered in 1998, falling 16 percent to 1,619. Although senior management steadfastly maintained that the new models would not appear before the end of the century, it was clear that replacements would have to arrive much sooner than that. And they did—in 1998.

Meanwhile, the possibility of Rolls-Royce ownership being transferred to a German company brought about something of a catfight between BMW and Volkswagen and raised uncertainties in the marketplace. One question already on the minds of Rolls-Royce and Bentley lovers centered on whether the essence and the exclusivity would be lost with BMW engines in the cars.

Some customers decided to wait on the sidelines. With the new Silver Seraph and Bentley Arnage due to launch in March 1998, and the Silver Spur continuing limited production as a hedge against lukewarm reaction, the company was looking for sales of about 2,500. Fears of low sales were realized, and estimates were revised downward several times. What should have been a banner year, with the largest profit for nine years, was little short of disastrous.

Not only that, but Rolls lost its recently arrived chief executive, Graham Morris, a very capable and highly regarded manager in the car industry. He quit in disgust at the horse trading and backroom deal-making between the parent company Vickers, BMW, and the owners of the Rolls-Royce trademark, Rolls-Royce plc, the aerospace company.

The character of the motor cars, of course, had changed. They had an overdue, less angular shape and new interiors, but most telling was that many of the mechanicals were now supplied by BMW. The company known throughout the world for its engineering no longer had an engine-building shop. BMW were contracted to supply engines for the new models—the Rolls-Royce Silver Seraph, and a 350-horsepower, 4.4-liter, V-8 turbocharged unit for the Bentley Arnage. (The Turbo R—now called the RT—retained its shape, and the

old 6.75-liter V-8—now built by Cosworth—retained its power base for 1999 with 400 horsepower.)

New five-speed transmissions, new suspensions, more body stiffness, and attractive new interior furnishings, along with a shapely new body, made for a sexy new pair on the block, although early customer feedback lamented the tightness of rear passenger space.

Sales expectations were not realized. The wealthy didn't get that way by being stupid or making a purchase without questioning its validity. And there were some who took the view that, despite the fact that Rolls-Royce engineers had worked with BMW on the

BELOW • Enhancements to the Bentley Turbo R 1996 model provided a power curve taking the 5310 lb. car from zero to sixty in under 5 seconds. The exterior was rounded and reshaped here and there, and the radiator shell downsized slightly.

engines, the units were basically BMW powerplants that retained even the unmistakable sound of a German engine. And in the United States some hesitated to pay well over $200,000 for a Rolls propelled by an almost identical engine to that in the $90,000 BMW 750il.

Amid all the car-launch activity in 1998, the power game was being played out. BMW, still keen to acquire Rolls-Royce, assumed it had the inside track, having an aerospace partnership in Europe with Rolls-Royce plc, the trademark owners. BMW made a low-ball offer—£150 million, at which price they could have been prosecuted for grand theft auto. As Volkswagen sniffed around, the offer was doubled to £300 million. Vickers accepted.

Then VW drove in from left field, with a move that shocked their rivals, topping the BMW offer with £530 million. And VW added £120 million for Cosworth Engineering, also part of the Vickers stable. A group of Rolls enthusiasts, desperate to keep Rolls-Royce British, tried to come up with a counter offer, but didn't get their act together in time, and a special shareholders' meeting voted for the VW bid.

A furious Bernd Pischetsrieder, BMW's chairman, threatened to stop supplying engines for the new cars. And he turned to Sir Ralph Robins, chairman of Rolls-Royce plc, to put the bite on, to point out that no one could use the Rolls-Royce name or the famous double-R badge without his company's permission. That would effectively prevent VW marketing any cars named Rolls-Royce. Then the brawl started, and VW, facing the prospect of having a car without an engine, backed down, and agreed to hand over the Rolls-Royce name to BMW in 2003. The cars might then be built at a separate factory.

BMW announced it had acquired the Rolls-Royce name for £40 million, the deal having VW produce both

Rolls and Bentleys for five years at the Crewe factory, then being left with just Bentley.

Meanwhile, with all the uncertainty about whether Rolls would have engine-less orphans on its hands with the just-launched new models, sales dropped by 30 percent, exactly when they should have been winding up.

The Rolls chief executive, Graham Morris, a former senior Rover man and latterly with VW/Audi, where he had a seat on the Audi board, had taken up his new post a little over a year earlier. Pleased with the prospect of much-needed investment from his old company, he felt able to promise the Rolls workforce that new ownership by VW would give the company a strong, stable future.

Astonishingly, Morris was kept in the dark about the goings-on between London, Munich, and Wolfsburg. He told me later he was left with no alternative to resignation, having given an assurance to the workers that production of Rolls-Royce cars would remain at Crewe. VW flew him to Germany to ask that he change his mind. He refused, but agreed to stay on for a few more months, until Christmas 1998, while a new CEO was found to replace him.

After several months, a senior engineer at the Crewe factory, Tony Gott, who had been in charge of the Seraph project, was made acting CEO, and in April 1999, he was confirmed as chief executive.

AND THE FUTURE?

It is difficult to speculate with deep conviction about the future of Rolls-Royce Motor Cars Ltd. The management, conscious that it loses ownership of the Rolls-Royce brand in 2003, is bound to focus its energies on Bentley and where to take the brand. Bentley sales have outpaced Rolls-Royce for several years, drivers preferring the sportier, more performance-oriented cars bearing the lower-profile grille.

But the Germans will have to thread their way delicately through a minefield. They might do well to take a leaf from Ford's book. When it bought Jaguar—a marque suffering many more problems than those besetting Rolls-Royce—it was careful to inject all the engineering expertise and marketing muscle needed to develop attractive and reliable products, while allowing the quintessential Britishness of the Jaguar to continue to dominate. It worked.

There will always be some customers around who desire the ultimate status symbol—a Rolls-Royce—a motorcar whose beautifully crafted wood and leather interior is unmatched by any other car on the planet (unless it be a Bentley). And, with BMW in charge of the engineering, it will reach reliability standards previously unknown. But we are living in changing times where a high profile is not always desirable. It will be interesting to see how BMW tackles the job of trying to raise Rolls sales and showing a profit without changing the character of the car.

The same applies to Bentley. Soon after assuming ownership, VW talked of building 9,000 Bentleys a year, which some might consider a severe dilution of much of its appeal—its exclusivity.

So long as both Rolls-Royce and Bentley motor cars continue to be built in England, and the world's finest craftsmen and -women make the interiors—and so long as the vehicles have the traditional feel of Crewe-built cars—they will survive.

Some speculate that both BMW and VW, whose expertise at what they do is unquestioned, may find it difficult—may even be frustrated—as they try to embrace or understand the unique qualities inherent in the Rolls-Royce company and its products. And, with the powerful profit motivation that drives mass car makers, they may throw up their hands after a few years and seek to return Rolls and Bentley to British ownership. Whatever the pressures and the problems, there has to be a place in the automotive world for these special products that exemplify traditional British craftsmanship, and a romantic story worth preserving.

I think these motorcars will endure.

INDEX